MANAGEMENT BY MISSIONS

MANAGEMENT BY MISSIONS

Pablo Cardona

and

Carlos Rey

palgrave
macmillan

First published 2008 by
PALGRAVE MACMILLAN
Houndmills, Basingstoke, Hampshire RG21 6XS and
175 Fifth Avenue, New York, N.Y. 10010
Companies and representatives throughout the world

PALGRAVE MACMILLAN is the global academic imprint of the Palgrave Macmillan division of St. Martin's Press, LLC and of Palgrave Macmillan Ltd. Macmillan® is a registered trademark in the United States, United Kingdom and other countries. Palgrave is a registered trademark in the European Union and other countries.

ISBN-13: 978–0–230–55152–7
ISBN-10: 0–230–55152–1

This book is printed on paper suitable for recycling and made from fully managed and sustained forest sources. Logging, pulping and manufacturing processes are expected to conform to the environmental regulations of the country of origin.

A catalogue record for this book is available from the British Library.

A catalog record for this book is available from the Library of Congress.

10 9 8 7 6 5 4 3 2 1
17 16 15 14 13 12 11 10 09 08

Printed and bound in China

Contents

Contents

Foreword

The management by missions (MBM) model presented in this book rests on three pillars: theoretical research (literature study), practical research (field study), and implementation consulting (practical application in companies).

The first pillar, theoretical research, is the one that answers the following questions: Has anybody written anything on this subject before? What theories or views have they put forward? We soon realized that, besides the literature we already had in our library, there is a wealth of publications bearing directly or indirectly on the subject of this book. We carried out an in-depth literature analysis on issues such as mission, values, culture, motivation, quality, processes, leadership, and so on.

The second pillar of our model is practical research. Initially, in a study carried out in 2000 based on a questionnaire sent to 220 companies, we identified the various relationships between corporate culture and profit. In 2002, we carried out a second study focused on companies' experiences of defining and implementing a corporate culture. In total, we have collected more than 1300 mission statements and values statement from companies around the world. We have used them to determine the main characteristics of what might be termed a "healthy corporate culture."

Lastly, since 2003, we have been conducting a third study: a large-scale, in-company study carried out through the International Research Center on Organizations (IRCO) at IESE. To date, more than 100 organizations and more than 6000 managers and middle managers have taken part in this study. Thanks to their collaboration, we have been able to explore the main problems facing companies today and gather a wide range of experiences and ideas about "what to do" and "what not to do" in order to create a successful corporate culture.

The third pillar of our MBM model, implementation consulting, is what enabled us to publish this book with the certainty that the proposals and ideas it contains have been tried and tested and actually work in practice. As a result, over the last five years we have tested the ideas and solutions described in this book in companies of all sizes in different industries.

This book consists of three parts, and the third part is concluded by a practical case in which we explain in detail how a company, Sony Spain, has used MBM to implement a cultural change. The three pillars – theoretical research, practical research, and implementation consulting – are combined in all three parts of the book. In each part, however, they are combined in different proportions.

- The first part has a greater theoretical content. In this part we explore prevailing assumptions about what a company is and what it is for. Specifically, we discuss the problems and limitations we have observed in modern corporations. This first part, which may seem dry, is crucially important as it contains the key to a deeper understanding of the following two parts.

- The second part is based mainly on our practical research. In this part we reflect on the main deficiencies and limitations of existing corporate cultures and describe what a corporate culture is, how a mission is defined, what values are most sought after, how to define a "healthy" corporate culture, and so on.

- The third part is primarily the result of our consulting work. In it we present the main tools of MBM and the type of leadership needed to implement it. These tools and the leadership style we describe mark a path toward a new management model and a new way of understanding the work that managers do.

Our aim in this book is not to provide definitive solutions to management problems. Nor do we intend this to be an instruction manual on "how to manage a company." The book is a preliminary proposal about a new way of understanding management. We want to draw attention to the need for a change in today's management models. We hope that this book will help managers learn how to create a high-commitment culture by adding value to people's work and organizing their efforts in an increasingly efficient and motivating way.

Part I

Myths and Realities of Management

1

Is there a link between corporate culture and profit?

In his well-known book *The Human Equation*,[1] Jeffrey Pfeffer demonstrates, with numbers and logic, that companies can earn much higher profits (more than 30 percent higher) if they adopt management practices that increase people's commitment and competence. This claim seems to hold true for different types of industries (from steel to semiconductors), for a wide variety of companies (from manufacturing to services), and for diverse business strategies across the cost-differentiation spectrum. As Arie de Geus illustrates in an article, "The Living Company,"[2] firms that have survived for more than a century acquire certain common characteristics, which are precisely the ones that have enabled them to adapt to major, even radical, changes in the political, social, and economic environment. One of those characteristics is the ability to build a community of managers and employees who are committed to the company as a long-term venture.

These studies show clearly and systematically that high performance and long-term survival both depend to a large extent on the nature and depth of employees' commitment to the enterprise. There is nothing new about this. What may be new, though, at least to some, is the evidence supporting it. Today more than ever, companies need committed employees in order to compete successfully in the international environment. The impact of management decisions on employees' commitment therefore deserves more attention. Just as strategy deals with the economic consequences of management decisions, we propose a new term, "intrategy," to describe the impact of management decisions on employees' commitment to the company.

More specifically, intrategy is the study of a company's environment and internal processes. It is aimed at strengthening people's commitment to the company and trust in its management. Intended or not, every management decision has a strategic consequence – an increase or decrease in profit – and an intrategic consequence, namely a strengthening or weakening of people's commitment to and trust in the company. Any decision made taking only one of these two consequences into account is, to say the least, incomplete, if not a threat to the company's business and survival.

Unity: The bottom line of corporate culture

Management professors, on the one hand, and business owners and managers, on the other, often talk about corporate culture as if it were different from, though related to, companies' financial performance. We have a clear measure of financial performance, profit, which can be calculated in many different ways: return on investment (ROI); return on equity (ROE); return on sales (ROS) and so on. As an indicator, profit is very useful for making decisions and assessing management performance. The cultural dimension of performance, by contrast, is much more difficult to judge, precisely because there is no obvious way of measuring it.

Many managers ask themselves, with good reason, "Is it possible to measure anything so complicated and subjective?" At first sight, we may feel there are just too many factors affecting people's behavior in companies. Luckily, most studies on this subject come to the same conclusion: the root and essence of a company's culture is the mutual trust and commitment between the company and its employees. Trust and commitment are mutually reinforcing: one cannot exist without the other, as they are basically two sides of the same coin, which we call "unity."

Unity is necessary for the life of any social body or organization and is not to be confused with the rigidity that impedes change, that is, uniformity.

A uniform body is most often a dead body. Living organisms are composed of very diverse members, which interact continuously, providing the various inputs required to achieve a common goal. Diversity and interdependence are necessary conditions for true unity, and unity is a condition of life. When an organism loses unity, it starts to decompose. That is why long-lived companies typically have a high degree of unity. We define unity as the degree of mutual trust and commitment between the company and the people who work in it. This definition applies to any level of the company: division, department or group.

In management literature, companies that have a high degree of unity are known by a variety of names: "excellent companies,"[3] "high trust organizations,"[4] "citizen corporations,"[5] "the individualized corporation,"[6] and so on. With slight variations in emphasis, all these companies have policies that increase their employees' mutual trust and commitment. Thus, unity can be seen as a precise and useful "bottom line" for cultural performance: a simple criterion to assess the effectiveness of management decisions in the cultural dimension.

Although there is no standard measure of unity, there are various ways of assessing it. One way is in terms of "organizational commitment."[7] *Fortune* magazine uses a measure called "The Great Place to Work Trust Index" to select the top 100 companies in different countries in terms of employees' trust in management, pride in their work and their company, and camaraderie. This comes fairly close to what we have called "unity."

Unity and survival

The organizations ranked among *Fortune*'s 100 best companies to work for have high levels of unity. According to Arie de Geus, that makes them likely candidates to survive longer than other companies in the same competitive environment. Among others things, it is because they are able to adapt more quickly and more successfully to changes in the environment. As a Hewlett-Packard (HP) executive said a few years ago,

> At Hewlett-Packard, we experienced major changes when we went from being an instrumentation company to being a computer company. I think the level of trust in HP allows us to move very quickly in restructuring the way we operate. That is a significant advantage compared to other companies that have to make a great effort to change and then are only partly successful. In HP, the level of trust is high enough for people to believe that they will not suffer as a result of change.[8]

Companies with high levels of unity are better able to adapt to changes in the environment, because it takes trust to foster individual initiative, knowledge transfer, and organizational learning – things on which any organizational change depends. It is confirmed by the experience of companies that have managed to create an intelligent organization. 3M is one of them. With revenues of more than 14 billion dollars and a history going back nearly 100 years, 3M is an example of a long-lived, high-performance company. Ghoshal and Bartlett believe that trust is at the heart of such performance:

> Trust was a clear element in the culture of all the companies we studied in which the knowledge transfer and organizational learning were at the heart of their strategic capability. At 3M, for example, a strong trusting relationship between senior managers and those in the front lines provided the context for individual initiative, while a shared confidence among those who worked together across organizational boundaries framed the environment for interunit support.[9]

Unity and profit

Unity and profit are connected in various ways, but they cannot be reduced to a single dimension. Successful companies need to strive for both. William Pollard, chairman and CEO of the ServiceMaster Company, expressed this idea in the following terms:

> If we focused exclusively on profit, we would be a company that has forgotten to feed its soul. Companies which do that experience a loss of direction and purpose among their people, a loss of customers, and eventually a loss of profit. Both people and profit are part of our mission.[10]

There are at least two confusions that may arise when people try to oversimplify the relationship between unity and profit. The first arises from the naive assumption that unity and profit are directly linked. Managers who take this approach think that if employees are more committed, the company is bound to be more profitable. Numerous studies have shown that unity, by itself, is not enough to explain differences in profit. Employees also need to have the right competencies, and the company must have a strategy appropriate to its specific competitive environment. This naive approach, which we call the "fallacy of the lily," may lead to opportunistic strategies, in which unity is simply a means of making a profit. Often, such strategies fail because they give priority to short-term opportunity costs and end up reducing the company's unity (without increasing profit).

The second confusion results from a false dichotomy between unity and profit. This approach assumes that there is an inverse relationship between unity and profit. Managers who adopt this approach, which we could call the "fallacy of the ax," think that strengthening employee commitment is expensive and so will reduce profit. In doing so, they fall into the same trap as companies used to, before the 1980s, with respect to cost and quality. As quality was assumed to be inversely proportional to cost, managers often accepted low quality products in the name of cost improvement. Although sacrificing product quality is an easy way to cut costs, it is clear today that companies can improve quality and cut costs at the same time. In fact, many companies that failed to do so have already been forced out of business. The same applies to the supposed dichotomy of unity and profit. The best companies, the ones that will survive in the years to come, are the ones that learn to increase both unity and profit at the same time. As Pfeffer has shown, if companies with a high degree of unity are able to align their management practices with their strategy, they may also earn higher profits.

Profit and unity are measures of two competitive dimensions that are fundamental to any company. Profit measures a company's economic relationship with its environment, while unity measures the company's internal state and its capacity for change and survival. For a complete diagnosis of a company's competitive position we must therefore take both dimensions into account. These dimensions can be represented in a two-by-two matrix. Given the way unity, profit, and survival are related, however, the competitive positions available to companies within the matrix are limited. As the limits mark out the shape of a funnel, we call this matrix the "Company Diagnosis Funnel (CDF)" (Figure 1.1).

The shape of the funnel may vary for different industries and periods, but the basic structure remains the same. Companies with higher levels of unity may subsist with lower levels of profit and so have a better chance of survival in times of crisis. Companies such as HP might have found it a lot more difficult

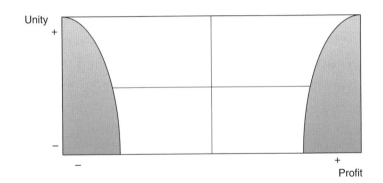

Figure 1.1 The funnel of unity and profit

to survive in the 1980s if they had not had such high unity. As it was, they were able to cut wages and develop new products, instead of being pulled into a dynamic of escalating layoffs that often ends in what Pfeffer, citing the example of Apple in the 1990s, called "the spiral of declining performance."

On the other side of the funnel, companies with higher unity can earn higher profits, given that lower commitment and trust lead to high transaction and monitoring costs, poor communication with lower levels, and weak identification with the strategy designed by top management. With the best conceivable strategy and a certain amount of good luck, a company with a low level of unity may make a decent profit. But the profit will be meager compared to what it might have obtained with a higher level of unity.

A company may be positioned anywhere in the funnel but, within that space, its position will not be not static. Rather, it will vary dynamically as the company's managers make decisions, its people develop new competencies, and the competitive environment changes. For example, the top ten companies in the 1998 *Fortune US* ranking included Southwest Airlines, Microsoft, Merck, and HP. Of these, only Southwest Airlines was still in the top ten in 2001. To maintain a high level of unity and profit, a company must continuously make good economic and organizational decisions.

The basic theses of the CDF model are as follows:

1. Companies may move to any part of the funnel by virtue of their own decisions and changes in the environment. In other words, there is no one-to-one correlation between unity and profit. This thesis refutes both the fallacy of the lily (positive correlation between unity and profit) and the fallacy of the ax (negative correlation).

2. There are certain areas of the profit–unity matrix in which we are unlikely to find any companies. These are the shaded areas outside the funnel in Figure 1.1.

Verification of the model

In the 1990s, two Harvard professors, Kotter and Heskett, conducted a study of the relationship between culture strength and business performance.[11] In their study, they took 207 companies from 22 different industries and measured the above-mentioned

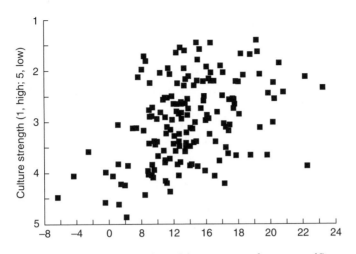

Figure 1.2 Culture strength and business performance (*Source*: Corporate Cultures and Performance)

two variables over a ten-year period. The results, using ROE as an indicator of economic performance, are shown in Figure 1.2. The bilateral correlation between culture strength and profitability is slightly positive (0.31), but not statistically significant.

For our part, in Spain, we carried out an empirical study with 220 companies, from which we chose 76 belonging to the following industries: food, machinery, pharmaceuticals, electronics, chemicals, and services.

To verify the basic theses of the CDF model described in the previous section, our study departed from Kotter and Heskett's model in two ways. On the one hand, we measured the cultural dimension using unity as our variable.[12] On the other, we compared the sample companies' performance (average three-year ROE) with the industry average in order to obtain a normalized value on the matrix's profit scale: positive if the average three-year ROE was above the industry average, negative otherwise. The normalized value of the average three-year ROE helps to highlight the ties between profit and unity that give rise to the funnel.

The results of our study are shown in Figure 1.3. Again, the bilateral correlation between unity and profit is slightly positive (0.16), but not statistically significant. In both studies, therefore, the model's first thesis is confirmed: unity and profit are not correlated, either positively or negatively. Companies with higher unity are not necessarily either more or less profitable than others.

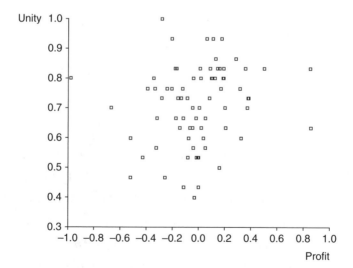

Figure 1.3 Unity and profit

Furthermore, the corrections we made in our study allow us to observe the prohibited spaces of the funnel in more detail: particularly if we look at Figure 1.3, we can see that there are fewer companies in the two lower corners, as our second thesis predicts. As unity increases, companies may occupy a larger space within the matrix.

Corporate cultures

As we said at the beginning, the great majority of management decisions affect both profit and unity. It would therefore be a mistake to take *only* strategic or *only* intrategic consequences into account when making management decisions. Moreover, no strategy, not even the best strategy, would be any use without capable and committed people to put it into effect. Depending on the way their managers make decisions, companies acquire different cultures. Specifically, in the funnel in Figure 1.1, we can distinguish four types of corporate culture: paternalistic, bureaucratic, aggressive, and competent. This typology is depicted in Figure 1.4.

The managers of paternalistic companies make decisions that generate high levels of unity, but not high profit. The managers of aggressive companies make decisions that help achieve reasonable economic performance, but at the cost of unity. The managers of bureaucratic companies make decisions that generate neither profit nor unity. And the managers

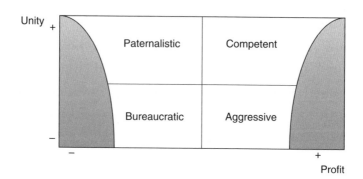

Figure 1.4 Culture's classification

of competent companies make decisions that produce high levels of unity and high profit at the same time.

This typology is consistent with Kotter and Heskett's qualitative study of companies situated at the extremes of the matrix. After studying these companies' history and development in depth and interviewing many of their managers and employees, Kotter and Heskett came to the following conclusions.

The companies with a strong culture and low profitability (paternalistic companies) are ones that were successful in the past. In all cases, the poor economic performance is attributable to an inability to adapt to major changes in the market, or the emergence of new competitors. As described by Kotter and Heskett, these companies have a culture centered on past achievements and steeped in complacency. Many of the respondents, when asked what gave their company its strong culture, said that they did.

The companies with a weak culture and high profitability (aggressive companies) hold a dominant position in their industry, sheltered by high entry barriers for new competitors or a legal setup that gives them exceptional competitive advantages. In light of their data, Kotter and Heskett conclude that it is indeed possible to achieve good performance with a weak culture, but only in environments "protected" by monopoly or oligopoly conditions.

The companies with a strong culture and high profitability (competent companies) have two basic characteristics that set them apart from the others in the sample. On the one hand, they have a culture centered on what Kotter and Heskett identify as key stakeholders: customers, shareholders, and employees. On the other, they have supervisor–subordinate relationships based, at all levels, on leadership.

Critical dynamics of cultural development

As we said earlier, companies do not remain in a fixed position within the funnel; unless they specifically do something to prevent it, they lose ground in both dimensions (profit and unity). In other words, companies must constantly make the right strategic and intrategic decisions merely to stay in the same place.

Another phenomenon that has become quite common in today's increasingly competitive and global environment is what we might call the "inverted z" dynamic. We can see it at work in competent companies that become less competitive at the economic level (due to technological change, the entry of new international competitors, etc). Over a period, the company slips into the paternalistic zone, until "steps are taken" to redress the situation. The change can be quite sudden if the now paternalistic firm is taken over by another company.

To illustrate, we can picture a Spanish company that at one time was competent, but has since become paternalistic, until one fine day it is bought up by a US multinational. A thrusting young executive is sent over from New York to breathe new life into the company. Experience shows that the Spanish company is very likely to shift toward the aggressive area of the funnel. This is because the only thing the bosses in New York measure is financial performance, and the easiest way to progress in that dimension is downward (as we saw with the cost–quality relationship).

If the company recovers economically, even at the cost of losing its unity, the executive will be rewarded. Quite likely he will be promoted back to headquarters, where more and more managers who can engineer this kind of abrupt turnaround congregate (thus reinforcing that particular style of management). The problem is that the company has fallen into a trap: increasing profit at the cost of unity is not a sustainable proposition. Once unity falls below a certain level, the company may start to lose vital talent: people will no longer recognize the company as their own and so will decide to move on. When that happens, some companies may find their financial performance starting to suffer.

The fact is that it is very difficult to steer companies toward the competent quadrant in a competitive environment where the only outcome of decisions that is measured is the economic outcome. Gradually, more and more companies drift toward the aggressive quadrant, thinking they are doing well because they are earning money. They do not stop to consider what they are failing to earn (not only at the economic level) as a result of not being truly competent. In small companies, a good general manager may be able to run his company successfully by doing everything himself. In medium-sized companies, however (and even more so in large ones), top managers need proper systems for measuring and assessing the cultural as well as the financial dimension.

Shared priorities

It is impossible to consistently generate unity in a company unless there is a shared mission and shared values that go beyond pure economic performance. Opportunistic strategies aimed at short-term economic benefit do not produce unity but aggressiveness and even cynicism. There are many examples to show that the managers of high-performance, long-lived companies have a strong sense of mission, looking beyond profit maximization.

In an interview conducted in 1992, John Young, then CEO of HP, observed,

> Maximizing shareholder wealth has always been a very secondary concern. Although profit is a cornerstone of what we do – it is a measure of our contribution and a means of self-financed growth – it has never been an end in itself.[13]

The cultural decline suffered by HP in recent years is notorious. In the new culture, which turned to be very different from the one described by Young, much greater emphasis was placed on maximizing economic performance. The results were plain to see. Contrary to conventional wisdom, maximizing profit is not a good priority, not even for shareholders; at least, not in the long run.

That is why our model is based on priorities shared by all the stakeholders of the company. More and more companies are choosing to define a mission that looks beyond economic profit. These companies need managers who fully identify with that mission and are capable of acting upon the organization to secure genuine commitment from its employees. For that reason, the ability to generate unity within an organization has become a highly sought-after leadership competency. Just as the goal of realizing people's greatest potential (through empowerment) signified a change in the conception of the managerial role in the last century, the quest for unity (also known as ownership or sense of belonging) signifies a revolutionary change in management today.

2

Different ways of understanding an organization

Since the industrial revolution, a variety of management theories and systems have emerged. For decades, academics, consultants, practicing managers, and experts in disciplines such as psychology or engineering have tried to answer the basic question: what is a company?

The various theories and currents of thought that have emerged over the years have produced a variety of perspectives and viewpoints, all of which have shaped the conception of the business enterprise that prevails in the world of management today. Broadly speaking, these perspectives may be classified into the following groups, ordered chronologically:

1. *Mechanical perspective*: The company is seen as a "machine" which must be managed "scientifically" through what might be termed the "rationalism" of planning and supervision.

2. *Organic perspective*: The company is seen as a "living organism" that has initiative and creativity, and that must be managed based on people's performance and abilities.

3. *Cultural perspective*: The company is seen as a "social organization" that has purposes and values, and whose managers must create a culture that ensures commitment and identification among its employees.

The prevailing idea or conceptual model of the company strongly influences the way any management system develops. That is why we want the management system proposed in this book to be founded on a solid conceptual model. Often, a well-prepared, broad-based conceptual model is as important as the actual solutions offered.

Next, we shall look at each of the above three perspectives in more depth and show how they can be unified in a single model, which we shall call the "integral model of the company."

Mechanical perspective

In the late nineteenth and early twentieth centuries, initiatives and theories based on "rationalism" flourished, giving rise to what is known as "scientific management." The main contributors were the German sociologist Max Weber and the American engineer Frederic Taylor. Weber stated that bureaucracy was the most efficient form of human organization, while Taylor maintained that people's activity could be studied systematically and broken down into its elementary parts. For Taylor, managing a company consisted basically of planning and supervising activities:

> The work of every workman is fully planned out by the management at least one day in advance, and each man receives in most cases complete written instructions, describing in detail the task which he is to accomplish, as well as the means to be used in doing the work.[1]

During the first half of the twentieth century, Taylor's ideas spread throughout the world and were introduced to Europe by experts such as Urwick, in England, and Fayol, in France. Fayol, in particular, developed a definition of management that reflects very well his contemporaries' thinking: "to manage is to plan, organize, command, coordinate, and control."[2]

This "rationalistic" current of thought focuses on the basic elements of what we have called "the mechanical perspective" (Figure 2.1). Those elements are strategy, processes, and resources.

According to this perspective, managing a company consists of developing a successful strategy,

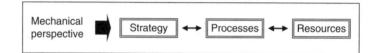

Figure 2.1 Mechanical perspective

implementing it appropriately through certain processes (manuals, procedures, policies, rules, etc.), and
using resources (revenues, capital, debt, expenditure,
working capital, and investment) efficiently. A company's profitability, return, and financial health, and
also its capacity to undertake new strategies in the
future, will depend on how successfully these three
elements are administered and aligned. For decades,
this simple and direct way of understanding the corporation was the basis for management techniques and
models.

The most widely used of these, introduced in the 1970s
and still in use today, include budgeting systems, job
descriptions, and strategic planning models. Such tools
allow managers to specify the company's goals in
terms of tasks, action plans, and procedures, which can
then be distributed throughout the organization.

Broadening Fayol's definition and adapting it to the
strategic requirements of today's world, it would be
fair to say that, under the mechanical perspective,
managing a company consists of the following:

1. analyzing the environment and the resources available to set strategies and goals,

2. making detailed plans, and lastly,

3. implementing processes and monitoring resources.

A good manager, therefore, is one that is good at
designing successful strategies, implementing them

by repeatedly executing processes, and husbanding the company's resources, especially its human resources, all the while carefully planning and supervising activities, roles, and responsibilities.

The leadership style associated with this perspective is "management by tasks." This is the typical "command and control" style of the manager who relies on strict task allocation and fully centralized decision making to keep his people in line. This way of managing people has some advantages: it is orderly and well planned, and in certain environments even efficient. It has major shortcomings, however. For one thing, it smothers initiative and creativity, so that people perform well below par.

One of many real-life examples is that of the head of one of a Swiss automotive supplier's manufacturing facilities. All his direct reports had clear instructions to seek his approval before doing anything that was not strictly planned. He was almost obsessive in his desire for control. He worked long hours to supervise all three shifts, and insisted on making all the decisions himself. Denied initiative and creativity, his subordinates found their work purely mechanical: reporting incidents and awaiting instructions.

Organic perspective

In the 1930s, Harvard psychologist Elton Mayo carried out various studies on the influence of certain external factors on worker productivity.

The best-known example is the study of lighting conditions in Western Electric's Hawthorne plant. First, Mayo increased the light intensity in the workplace and observed that productivity increased. Subsequently, he decreased the light intensity and observed that productivity again increased. What was happening?

For a decade, Mayo carried out numerous similar studies with equally disconcerting results. In the end, he put forward the theory that the simple fact of paying attention to the workers, of asking them to take part in something they felt was important, greatly influenced their productivity. Mayo's experiments opened up a new line of psychologically based research and development, in which people were seen as the decisive factor in companies' success.

Following a similar approach, one of the most important contributions after World War II was Douglas McGregor's Theory X and Theory Y.[3] Each of these two theories gives a very different view of the worker. While Theory X states that the worker is lazy and needs constant supervision, Theory Y says that the worker is capable of being creative and innovative and will naturally seek responsibility. Through these two theories, McGregor called into question the idea that planning and supervision are the determining factors in the company's success.

In the second half of the twentieth century, under the influence of this view of the company, human resources took on an increasingly important role. That is because, although some human activity can be planned and controlled in the way the mechanistic theories suggest (formal activity), most of the work people do depends on initiative and creativity, and requires deeper personal involvement (qualitative activity).

Nowadays, automation and new technology have taken over most of the formal activity. As a result, fewer workers now perform purely formal tasks. A growing number of jobs add value through qualitative activity. The more complex the environment and the organization, the greater the need to provide an outlet for employees' initiative and creativity and create an attractive work environment (workplace climate), in which people can realize their full potential.

Based on the experience of successful companies, Pfeffer, in his book *The Human Equation*, lists seven key people management practices:[4] employment security, selective hiring, decentralized decision making, contingent compensation, training, reduction of status differences, and sharing of financial and performance information. Pfeffer stresses that for these practices to be effective, they must be consistent with one another and with the company's strategy.

Companies today are making serious efforts to create a pleasant climate for their employees. Successful practices include the following:

- *Profit sharing*: Employees of Merck, Procter & Gamble, and W.L. Gore have the opportunity to buy shares in their company.

- *Decentralized decision making*: "They treat you with respect, they pay you well, and they empower you. They use your ideas to solve problems" (an employee of Southwest Airlines).

- *Employment security*: Usually, around, 20 percent of the companies in the *US Fortune* 100 Best Companies to Work For list have a no-layoff policy. Others, such as Hallmark Cards and 3M, go to extraordinary lengths to avoid layoffs.

- *Hiring policies*: At Whole Foods Market, people have to be voted into their jobs by their future coworkers in order to become permanent employees. MBNA's number one selection criterion is "People who know how to treat people."

- *Extensive training*: Korning expects all its employees to devote 5 percent of their time to training. At Motorola, every employee – from the general manager down to the greenest recruit – must complete at least 40 hours of training a year.

- *Reduction of status differences*: The general manager of Intel works in an open cubicle. The general manager of Whole Foods Market earns a salary not more than ten times that of an average team member.

This new approach, which places the focus of management on people, constitutes what we have called

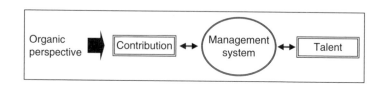

Figure 2.2   Organic perspective

"the organic perspective" (Figure 2.2). The organic perspective adds three fundamental elements to management: talent, management systems, and people's specific contribution (goals and results).

Giving people scope for initiative and creativity creates an organizational context that is richer but also more complex. Modern management systems arose in response to the need to cope with more complex environments. One of the first such management systems to be introduced was management by objectives (MBO), proposed by Peter Drucker in 1954[5] and implemented in numerous corporations. MBO is

> a process whereby the superior and subordinate managers of an organization jointly identify its common goals, define each individual's major areas of responsibility in terms of the results expected of him, and use these measures as guides for operating the unit and assessing the contribution of each of its members.[6]

Under MBO, each employee works in a context defined by objectives, for which he is responsible and which he accepts as challenges. The worker takes a proactive attitude toward achieving his objectives. Unlike "management by tasks," the focus of management is no longer on the task but on the results. This encourages managers to concentrate their efforts on the few activities that are capable of producing significant business results.[7]

Later, as a complement to MBO, came the philosophy of "empowerment": a context of autonomy and motivation, encouraging people to use creativity and initiative. Lawler,[8] one of the main proponents of this philosophy, defines empowerment in four dimensions: power, information, rewards, and knowledge (PIRK). Power consists of ensuring that people have sufficient power and resources to meet their targets. Information consists of giving people the information they need in order to achieve their objectives. Rewards has to do with the benefits and rewards workers may obtain if they accomplish their objectives. Knowledge consists of helping employees to acquire the knowledge and skills to do their job successfully.

Cultural perspective

In the early 1980s, after a decade marked by the oil crisis, poor business performance, and increasing competition worldwide, managers were looking for new ideas and solutions. Among the various currents of management thought prevailing at the time, three books caught the attention of practitioners and scholars: Ouchi's *Theory Z*,[9] Pascale and Athos's *The Art of Japanese Management*,[10] and Peters and Waterman's *In Search of Excellence*.[11] They all became best-sellers and were very influential, and still are today. *In Search of Excellence* remains one of the best-selling management books of all time.

These and other books based on studies of the world's most successful companies revealed, among other things, something that left much of the business world perplexed: the key to lasting success does not lie in particular strategies or efficient resource management, but in a hitherto largely ignored dimension of management, the cultural dimension.

Strictly speaking, cultural theories of the corporation were not a late-twentieth-century invention. Previously, various authors had written about the importance of corporate culture. The best-known of them is Chester Barnard,[12] who in the 1930s argued that one of the three primary functions of the executive is to formulate, define, and inculcate a common purpose that gives meaning to the organization. Barnard was not a theorist and cannot even be said to have developed a theory. Rather, he brought to bear his practical experience as president of AT&T, one of the United States' leading companies. A few other companies, such as HP, Johnson & Johnson, General Electric, and IBM, had similar experiences to that described by Barnard. But it was not until the 1980s that the cultural dimension started to attract serious attention in the world of management.

This current of thought incorporates a new way of understanding the company, the one we call "the

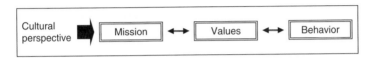

Figure 2.3   Cultural perspective

cultural perspective" (Figure 2.3). This perspective is made up of three elements, which together make up the core of an organization's culture: the mission, the values, and commitment that develop within the organization. These three elements are interrelated and so must be aligned in order to form a consistent culture. From the cultural perspective, a company is more than just a machine, or a group of people with initiative and creativity: it is a social institution with its own identity, defined by purposes and values that are shared by its members.

The cultural perspective aims to generate what might be termed "ownership" or a sense of belonging. Ownership goes beyond empowerment. In fact, many companies that have launched empowerment programs find that the difficult thing is not giving people more power, but gaining their commitment. To do this, companies must develop a culture that persuades people to identify with a shared undertaking and shared values.

This wish to obtain employee identification and commitment has led to a proliferation of attempts to develop a philosophy and a set of values that give meaning to business enterprise: the answer to the question of why companies exist. Nowadays, thousands of companies already have a formal mission and values statement, and the trend is steadily increasing. Meanwhile, internal communication departments and systems designed to spread such philosophies throughout the organization have mushroomed.

Various methods of building corporate cultures have emerged in recent years. These methods are based on creating models and symbols that reinforce the desired values. Some companies go further and award prizes to people who live their values to the full. Lastly, other companies have set up interfunctional groups to work on specific projects to promote certain values. And naturally, all these efforts are explicitly backed by top management and reinforced by a suitable internal communication campaign.

The integral model of the company

The three perspectives we have described are entirely complementary and necessary for any organization to develop and succeed. A company cannot be defined exclusively by any one of these perspectives; all three are required. The mechanical perspective provides the "rational logic" of planning and supervision that is needed for the company to operate. The organic perspective adds the creativity and initiative that takes the company beyond the limits of corporate planning. And the cultural perspective promotes internal unity through a common purpose that harnesses the commitment and identification of the employees.

In our research, we have found that many companies today are striving to integrate these three perspectives. Yet, a deep division persists within organizations. In practice, the culture that companies would like to have and the reality of day-to-day management very rarely coincide. The underlying problem is the dichotomy between the cultural perspective and the existing management systems: on the one hand, efforts are made to "build a culture" (communication, speeches, outdoor activities, awards, posters, etc.); on the other, oblivious to such efforts or even working against them, the management system judges people mainly on economic criteria.

To solve this problem we need to design and implement a new management system that combines all three perspectives in a single model, which we call "the integral model of the company" (Figure 2.4).[13]

As we shall see in Part II of this book, existing management systems – which take account of only the first two perspectives at best – are incapable of achieving such integration. That is why we need to

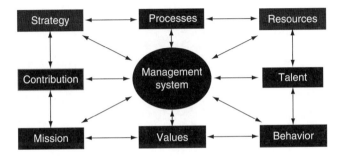

Figure 2.4 Integral model of the company

create a new management system that integrates the cultural perspective (mission, values, and commitment) in the company's day-to-day practice. Before we do that, however, in order to fully understand what an integral management system should look like, in the next chapter we shall consider the question of why the company exists: what is the true purpose of a business enterprise?

3

What are companies for?

It seems reasonable to assume that an organization and its members should have a clear idea of their purpose.[1] In practice, however, this is not always the case. Very often, there is great confusion and conflict of opinion on this point, even within the board of directors or the executive committee.

The basic problem, when a company does not have an explicit statement of common purpose, is that utilitarian or opportunistic theories are likely to prevail. According to these theories, a company has no purpose as such; what it does is simply the end result of the private interests of its members and the influence exerted upon it by various outside agents.

However, this opportunistic view precludes cooperation. As Barnard declared in the 1930s, without cooperation there can be no organization, and for there to be cooperation, there has to be a common purpose.

Willingness to cooperate, except as a vague feeling or desire for association with others, cannot develop without an objective of cooperation. Unless there is such an objective it cannot be known or anticipated what specific efforts will be required of individuals, nor in many cases what satisfactions to them can be in prospect.[2]

David Packard, one of the founders of HP, is a good example of how important it is to have a shared purpose. In 1960, 23 years after the company was founded, Packard began a speech at the opening of a management development program with the following words:

First of all, I'd like to talk about what companies are for. In other words, why are we here? I think a lot of people assume, wrongly, that companies exist simply to make money. Although profit is an important outcome of a company's activity, we need to look beyond that for the true reasons why companies exist. (...)

Looking around, one can still find people whose only interest is money, but the underlying motives come from the desire to do something more – make a product, render a service... basically, make something of value. With these thoughts in mind, let's consider why Hewlett-Packard exists.[3]

It is safe to say that, like HP, most companies that have made a serious effort to define their mission have started by asking themselves what they are there for. All the companies that have attempted it have found that defining a company's purposes is no simple task, especially if the company is owned or controlled by more than one person. Despite the difficulties, however, we have found no case in which it was felt to have been a waste of time: it is always worthwhile.

Profit: means or end?

The first problem we encounter when we try to define a company's purpose is understanding what role profit plays in the company's purpose. In the management literature, and also in the various interviews and conversations we have had with practicing managers, we have identified three different conceptions of the importance of profit.

The first sees profit maximization as the company's sole purpose. Ever since Adam Smith, there have always been those who declare that the company must confine itself exclusively to making a profit. Anything else a company does, they say, can only be understood as a means of making a profit. The best-known advocate of this view is Milton Friedman, who in the early 1960s stated, "There is one and only one social responsibility of business: to use its resources and engage in activities designed to increase its profits so long as it stays within the rules of the game, which is to say, engages in open and free competition without deception or fraud."[4] The issue is still discussed and debated in political, academic, and business circles today.[5]

The second way of understanding profit is that profit is one of several corporate purposes. Many people believe that companies should contribute more than just profit: they must render a service to individuals, groups, or society as a whole. In all it does, a company satisfies one or more needs of its various stakeholders: customers, employees, shareholders, suppliers, and members of the community in which it operates. Some contributions, such as the work done by a hospital, may seem more noble or enriching than that of, say, a bank. However, it is not our purpose in this book to make a moral judgment as to whether certain activities are better than others. The point we wish to make is that, for many companies, the contribution they make to their various stakeholders is an end in itself, on a par with making a profit. In fact, this is the interpretation we have found repeated most often in the mission statements of the more than 1300 companies we have analyzed.

The third way of understanding profit is that profit is not even an end in itself, but a means to other ends. "Profit is a necessary condition for existence and a means to more important ends, but for many visionary companies it is not an end in itself. Profit is as oxygen, food, water or blood are to the body; they are not the most fundamental things in life, but without them there can be no life."[6] This attitude is exemplified by Hallmark:

We believe that financial results are indispensable, not as an end in themselves, but as a means to fulfill our mission.

(Hallmark Cards Inc, Beliefs & Values)[7]

The danger of simplification

What is the company's purpose? To make money? Certainly, profit may be an objective for many companies. But is it the only one? As we have seen, defining the company in terms of a single purpose is one of the three possible responses to the problem, but in most cases it is an oversimplification. The main reason for such simplification is that it is usually easier to argue from a simple mental scheme than to sustain the necessary complexity. Because of such simplification, we tend consciously or unconsciously to associate the company with a single, absolute purpose. What is the company's purpose? To make money.

To avoid the trap of oversimplification, we need to start with a broader conception of the purposes of the company. Initially, an organization's ultimate purpose – why the company exists – is explained by several relative purposes, one of which is to make money. Building on this, we need to concentrate on the purposes that constitute the company's identity.

Oversimplifying the company's purposes, besides being a distortion of reality, may become an outright attack on the beliefs of many of the people who work for it. When profit is the sole purpose, everything else becomes a means. Imagine, for example, the case of a private hospital. Doctors would challenge us if we suggest that the sole purpose of their hospital is to "make money." If we are talking about a private hospital, the wrongness of our assumption is plain to see. In other cases, however, where the business activity does not have such a clear social dimension, as in the case of a bank or a trading company, the error may not be so obvious. It is no less an error, however, as the key point is not necessarily how socially motivated the activity is.

At the same time, defining profit as the company's sole purpose is not the only type of oversimplification. Statements such as "we exist to serve our customers" or "the company's true purpose is its people" can lead to the same mistake. Customers or people may be a company's purpose, but can they be the only one? As a rule, when phrases such as these are used, the aim is to highlight some particular strategic objective, rather than to make a formal statement of purpose. Nevertheless, it is important to think ahead and be careful when making such claims, as "catchphrases" like this often lead to inconsistencies and serve merely to arouse confusion and skepticism.

Henry Morgan, the author of Ben & Jerry's mission statement (one of the companies known worldwide for their missions), said in an interview, "Most missions that focus on just one aspect are unhelpful. That is why, for Ben & Jerry's, I wrote three missions:

the product mission, the economic mission, and the social mission."[8]

To avoid oversimplification, we need to overcome our natural inclination to see the purpose of the company as a dilemma: either one thing or the other. The key insight is precisely that this is not an either/or choice, but a quest for balance and complementarity. Understanding this, we can overcome the tyranny of "A or B" and start to think in terms of "A and B."[9] We then stop talking about a single purpose and talk instead about several purposes: profit, people, customers, shareholders, and so on.

It should be pointed out, however, that while the tyranny of "A or B" leads us inexorably to a single purpose, choosing "A and B and C and D" may lead to an infinite number of purposes. As one may imagine, assuming that the organization has one and only one purpose is as mistaken as assuming that everything the organization does is an end in itself.

Balance and complementarity

Accepting that the company has several purposes leads to a new problem: how to find the right balance and complementarity between different purposes. In principle, one might assume that all the purposes of a company should be given equal importance. As a rule, the answer is not that simple. Finding the right balance in each case is an important part of defining the company's mission.

In fact, finding this balance – which is the opposite of maximization – is key to the company's success. This is the conclusion we draw from the studies by Collins and Porras.[10] In their research (Figure 3.1), Collins and Porras compared top-performing companies ("visionary companies") with those whose performance was good but not outstanding ("comparison companies"). After analyzing the evolving traits of the two groups over a period of more than 80 years, they identified two fundamental characteristics that differentiate the top performers:

1. They preserve a mission and values that go beyond profit.

2. They stimulate change through continuous improvement and highly demanding and ambitious goals.

As described by Collins and Porras, the genius of visionary companies consists in having not just one or other of these two characteristics, but both at once! The key to success lies precisely in finding the right balance and complementarity between what, at first sight, may seem contradictory imperatives. Is it easy? Not at all. Is it impossible? Definitely not. There are plenty of successful companies to prove it.

We may wonder how these companies are able to combine diverse purposes. There is no simple answer, no one way of doing it. Instead, Collins and Porras discuss practices that have worked in some of these companies, such as creating deeply

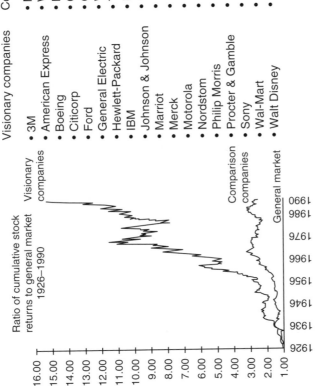

Comparison companies

• Norton
• Wells Fargo
• McDonnell Douglas
• Chase Manhattan
• GM
• Westinghouse
• Texas Instruments
• Burroughs
• Bristol-Myers Squibb
• Howard Johnson
• Pfizer
• Zenith
• Melville
• RJR Nabisco
• Colgate
• Kenwood
• Ames
• Columbia

Visionary companies

• 3M
• American Express
• Boeing
• Citicorp
• Ford
• General Electric
• Hewlett-Packard
• IBM
• Johnson & Johnson
• Marriot
• Merck
• Motorola
• Nordstrom
• Philip Morris
• Procter & Gamble
• Sony
• Wal-Mart
• Walt Disney

Ratio of cumulative stock
returns to general market
1926–1990

Visionary companies

Comparison companies

General market

Figure 3.1 Visionary and Comparison companies (*Source: Built to last*)

symbolic cultures. Ultimately, every company must find its own way of combining the different purposes that come into play when decisions are made. It would be much easier if the company had just one decision criterion: profit, for example. But such simplicity, besides impoverishing the decision process, would also impoverish the company's purpose and, with it, people's commitment to the enterprise.

Before ending this chapter, we shall set out a few definitions and basic rules to be followed when addressing the issue of balance and complementarity among a company's purposes. Specifically, we shall focus on what we mean by an organization's purpose and how that purpose is structured.

Organizational purpose

As we have seen, one of management's toughest challenges is finding the right balance and complementarity among the company's various purposes. From now on, we shall use the singular "purpose" to refer to a company's multiple purposes. Specifically, in talking about a company's purpose we shall be referring to the relationship of balance and complementarity among its various purposes. We do so in order to emphasize the fact that an organization's purposes are not separate and disjointed but a cohesive whole. An organization's purpose, therefore, is not the sum of a number of unrelated purposes that must be dealt with individually (sharing the effort out among them), but a rich and complex whole encompassing a variety of purposes which support and reinforce one another in many different ways.

Having defined the concept of purpose, we can now define an organization as a group of people whose actions are coordinated to achieve a common purpose. There are two fundamental and mutually necessary elements to this definition.

First, in any organization, activities are coordinated; this is what distinguishes a true organization from a simple group of people. The inhabitants of a city are a group of people; they are not an organization.

Second, the members of an organization share a common purpose. A hundred people working in a factory do not make an organization. Though they may all have very similar purposes (for example, doing their job properly), unless they share a common purpose, they are not, strictly speaking, an organization. Some authors even suggest that a company without a purpose is not a company at all; at best, we could call it "a business enterprise."[11]

Formally speaking, the members of a company are the people who work in it in an employment relationship based on the exchange of labor for money. For a person to be really – not just formally – a member of an organization, there has to be something more than a contractual relationship. A member of an organization is a person who, among the various personal motives and intentions that lead him to belong to the company, shares a common purpose with the rest of the members.

In our opinion, many companies have concentrated on coordinating goals and activities, while forgetting to simultaneously build a common purpose among their members. In other words, they have made huge efforts to ensure each person knows what he has to do, and even how to do it; but, with few exceptions, they have rarely given their employees the means to understand what they are working for.

Formulating an organization's purpose

A company's purpose is not just a matter for senior executives and company chairmen. Naturally, top managers must be the first to espouse a common purpose; but that purpose must filter down to every member of the organization, irrespective of rank, function, or length of service.

To communicate the purpose to the organization, it must be formulated in suitable terms. When formulating the corporate purpose, it is important to address two basic dimensions, both of which, as we saw in the first chapter, must be taken into account if we are to do justice to the reality of the company:

Intrategic dimension: This concerns that part of the corporate purpose that affects the company's culture and identity. It is commonly represented by two elements: mission and values.

Strategic dimension: This concerns that part of the corporate purpose that affects the company's competitive position in its environment. It is usually included in the concept of vision, which is an image of the future state we want to create or attain.[12]

Some companies talk about organizational purpose exclusively in terms of either the strategic or the intrategic dimension. Most, however, combine the two, using the three basic elements of organizational purpose: mission, vision, and values.

In Part II of this book, we shall focus on the intrategic dimension of corporate purpose. Specifically, we shall study the benefits and limitations of the corporate mission and values. We shall return to the strategic dimension in Part III, where we shall see how the two dimensions (intrategic and strategic) are combined and deployed throughout the organization.

Part II

In Search of Corporate Culture

4

Cultural problems today

It is not overdramatic to say that companies today – or at least, many companies in the Western world – are riven with contradictions. On the one hand, their philosophy and implementation of the corporate mission and values reflect what might be described as a humanistic vision, where the company is seen as a human institution, "the natural product of certain social needs."[1] On the other, their management systems, mostly built around management by objectives, are designed to maximize shareholder value. Everything else – customer service, talent development, even community donations – is a means to increase profit.

The more recent management tools aimed at enriching management by objectives, such as scorecards or competency management, tend to be adopted for essentially utilitarian reasons. The results are disheartening: implementation is slow and the expected benefits fail to materialize. Worst of all, this veiled tyranny of financial targets – often unintended, but nourished on a daily basis by management by objectives – slowly undermines employees' commitment to the company.

What kind of employees are going to feel enthusiastic about or committed to an enterprise that consists merely of maximizing shareholder value? Rather than commitment, what they feel is pressure, projected down the chain of command. Perceived as aggressive and unjustified, this pressure has a negative, paralyzing effect. People prefer to "keep their heads down" and shield themselves against the pressure from above by creating cushions that allow them to carry on "performing" at the expected level.

This incongruity we find in so many companies today has at least two undesirable consequences: the first is reduced cultural strength (ability to implement a corporate culture); and the second is reduced effectiveness of management by objectives, once the system has reached its ceiling.

Before discussing management by missions, which we shall do in the following chapters, in this section we shall put forward our personal view of these two problems. We shall present the results of research on companies' lack of cultural strength ("low-octane cultures"). And we shall describe the symptoms we have detected in many organizations, relating to the limits of management by objectives.

Low-octane cultures

Defining a culture (mission, values, principles, policies, etc.) is quite different from actually implementing it. We can judge how well established a culture is by its *cultural strength*, which has three basic dimensions.

1. *Commitment intensity*: This measures how thoroughly people know, and how closely they identify with, the company's mission.

2. *Cultural consistency*: This measures how well people know the company's values and priorities.

3. *Action capacity*: This measures whether the people in the company have the necessary motivation (attitude) and competencies (aptitude) to put the organization's culture into practice.

These three variables are the subject of a large-scale study we carried out on 108 companies (Table 4.1) of different sizes and in different industries, combining quantitative measurement (using questionnaires) with qualitative analysis (through personal interviews). Questionnaires were administered to a total of 6300 executives and middle managers, and 1750

Table 4.1 Distribution of sample companies

Manufacturing/ Services	Domestic/ International	No. of Employees	Total
Manufacturing	International	More than 500	6
		Less than 500	9
	Domestic	More than 500	3
		Less than 500	16
Services	International	More than 500	9
		Less than 500	18
	Domestic	More than 500	17
		Less than 500	30

interviews were conducted with employees at different levels. We found that although many companies have tried to develop a culture of their own, the results – in terms of *cultural strength* – are well below expectations.

We used the questionnaire results to measure cultural strength on a scale of 0–1, summing the scores in the three dimensions mentioned earlier (Figure 4.1). Only 8 of the 108 companies scored between 0.6 and 0.7. The average was 0.52 and a majority scored in the 0.4–0.6 range.

If we look at the three variables separately (Figure 4.2), the one with the lowest average score is cultural consistency (0.43), while commitment intensity scores 0.58, and action capacity, 0.56. This suggests that these companies have a lot of work to do in all three variables, and that the one needing most attention is cultural consistency.

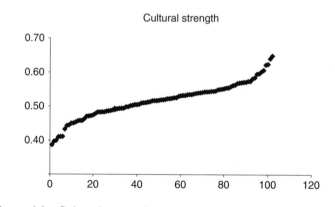

Figure 4.1   Cultural strength

Cultural strength	
	Aggregated
Commitment intensity	0.58
Cultural consistency	0.43
Action capacity	0.56
Total	0.52

Figure 4.2 Cultural strength aggregated

In the interviews, we discussed the results of each of the 108 companies with a random sample of employees at different levels in the hierarchy. The purpose of these roughly 45-minute interviews was to find out what were the main problems with the company's culture, as perceived by the company's top executives, middle managers, and front-line staff. Based on their responses, we selected the following as the most significant problems.

People do not really know the company's mission: Although many of the sample companies have formal mission statements, few employees really know what the mission is, and even fewer feel that it impacts on their daily work.

Lack of faith in the organization's values: Very often, the organizational values have no credibility. In many companies, employees are either unaware of them or see a discrepancy between what the company "preaches" and what it "practices."

Inadequate top-down communication: Most of the companies surveyed have communication tools (some even have communication departments), and yet communication is seen as inadequate or confusing, especially at lower levels of the organization.

Inadequate horizontal communication: Information does not flow naturally across departments. People regularly complain that departments do not want to share information. This makes life difficult for both sides. Some perceive this as an "invisible barrier" that makes areas opaque to one another.

Lack of cooperation: Each area is a silo; cooperation takes place only on certain preestablished issues, or when group work makes it inevitable. People do not proactively pursue cooperation. Everyone "does his own thing" and "only takes any notice" of others when he has a problem or is looking for someone to blame.

The final conclusion of our research is that "low-octane cultures" are the rule in companies today. Most companies invest a considerable amount of effort and resources in developing a corporate culture; and yet, there remains ample scope to implement this culture more effectively at all levels of the organization.

The limits of management by objectives

As we saw in earlier chapters, under MBO each employee's main areas of responsibility are defined in terms of the results he is expected to obtain. These expectations then serve as a guide to operations and a measure of each person's contribution. For a person to be able to contribute as agreed, his boss must delegate, or "empower" him, giving him the necessary resources, information, decision-making power, and knowledge. And if the person achieves the objectives, he must be rewarded accordingly. Originally, MBO was intended to encourage employees to act autonomously, using their initiative and creativity for the company's benefit. In theory, it was supposed to bring into play all the human potential that remained unexploited under traditional "command-and-control" management.

And yet, when MBO is implemented in a context in which employees are not personally committed to the company, employees tend to take the path of least resistance, using their objectives as an excuse and confining themselves to the agreed minimum. A typical example would be a sales rep who is expected to shift 100 units of a given product (say, cars) per year. If come November he finds he has already met his target with one month still to go before the end of the year, he has two options: take a month's vacation, or sell more cars. A good rep will carry on selling; but he will see to it that those "extra" sales do not show up until January. Why? Because if he tells his boss he has sold 115 cars this year, the target for next year will be 120, and the sales rep does not want to risk having such a high target. Instead, he will go to his boss in January with his target of 100 nicely met (and with 15 cars in reserve, to be reported once next year's targets have been negotiated).

It is not only at the lower levels of the organization that people try to give themselves this sort of sand bag. The sales rep's boss will very likely have his own sand bag, and so on upward. The consequence is that no manager three levels up knows what is really happening on the ground (much less a senior executive in a large corporation). Despite this, top management still tries – however hit-or-miss – to get the most out of the people below them, because they, too, are under pressure (and they, too, need to build a sand bag).

In these circumstances, instead of eliciting the greatest possible contribution from all employees, the system flounders in a vicious circle of wrangling over objectives. Employees will try to talk the objectives down, while top management will try to talk them up. Usually, the conflict is resolved by diktat from above and the introduction of external monitoring. This is a weakness of MBO that was noted as early as the 1950s by Drucker himself: "Our new ability to produce measurable information will enable self-monitoring; used in this way, it will lead to a huge gain in effectiveness and results. But if this new ability is abused to impose control from above, the new technology will cause incalculable damage and hamper management."[2]

For many companies, MBO is in fact an outdated system that cannot be expected to deliver more than

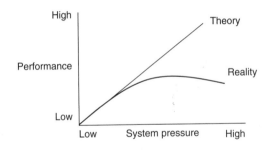

Figure 4.3 Performance and system pressure

incremental improvements on previous years' results. What's more, MBO has no answer to the question of employee commitment, as it is based on a dynamic that has no use for commitment. MBO establishes a direct relationship between system pressure and system performance (Figure 4.3): to get more profit, I have to use more pressure (which means higher incentives and harsher punishments). In the real world, however, this is true only for a while. Once the pressure reaches a certain level, people "take cover." And if the pressure is too high, they may even start to boycott the whole system. The most serious problem is that MBO can only increase results by increasing the pressure. And when the system is wound too tight, something may snap.

Judging by the results we see every day, MBO and empowerment have not come close to tapping employees' full potential. The main reason is that, without intense commitment, giving people more responsibility or power is futile; MBO becomes just another way of controlling them. In our opinion, although MBO and empowerment represent a major step forward in management, they get results only insofar as employees are committed. The problem today is not so much empowerment, as ownership: the sense of belonging, and the sense of mission.

Another consequence of MBO is that, given enough time and pressure, it eventually leads to a breakdown in communication within the company. In theory, MBO is intended to enhance communication and understanding up and down the hierarchy and across departments or units. The reality today is rather the opposite. People are constantly telling us, "I can't get through to my boss" (obviously not because the phone is out of order); "we work in silos"; and "what we need is a bit more team work."

If there is no awareness of a shared mission, MBO slowly breaks the company apart: up, down, and across the organization. On every rung of the hierarchical ladder, MBO creates potential enemies: the boss puts pressure on his subordinates and disbelieves everything they say. Subordinates do what they can to shield themselves and evade pressure at every turn. These subordinates themselves are bosses to other, lower-level employees. And so the same dynamic plays out again and again. Across the organization, MBO creates potential enemies among those who share interdependencies or processes. Sales complains that Production is too inflexible. Production complains that Planning gets its forecasts wrong. And Planning complains that Sales does not feed it the data on time. The company is fissured and increasingly unmanageable. Seventy years on, we are still banging our heads against Barnard's tautology: "Willingness to cooperate [. . .] cannot develop without an objective of coöperation."[3]

The drawbacks of objectives have been discussed by various experts, including W. Edwards Deming, one of the best-known advocates of quality systems:

> The idea of merit rating is alluring. The sound of the words captivates the imagination: pay for what you get; get what you pay for; motivate people to do their best, for their own good.
>
> The effect is exactly the opposite of what the words promise. Everyone propels himself forward, or tries to, for his own good, on his own life preserver. The organization is the loser.[4]

After so many years, the question remains the same: What is the objective of cooperation? So long as the corporate purpose continues to be (or continues to be perceived to be) exclusively to maximize shareholder value, companies will not realize people's full potential. Alternatives such as "corporate social responsibility" may generate a certain sense of mission and pride of belonging within an organization; but they do not affect management as such. This and other organizational initiatives will really hit home only if they are embedded in a mission that has content, credibility, and urgency.

Beyond management by objectives

We believe that the only way to overcome the limitations of MBO is by establishing a new organizational context in which people work with a sense of mission, that is, for transcendent motives. It is not a matter of exercising tighter control or piling on the pressure, but of getting people to feel more committed and motivated, so that they have a sharper sense of urgency and learn to raise their sights beyond strictly personal objectives. When people work with a sense of mission, they do not try to build a sand bag for themselves; nor do they content themselves with preestablished objectives. Even more importantly, they work naturally as a team.

This is not an unrealistic scenario, nor is it unattainable in practice. On the contrary, it is the context in which we humans naturally seek to freely realize our full potential. It is the context we find in family, friendship, or play. In contexts such as these, people feel united by a common purpose. They find it perfectly natural to strive for a common goal. That is because, maybe without realizing it, they are acting out of a sense of mission, an understanding of what it is all for, beyond satisfying their own extrinsic needs. It is sad to see how, in a business context ruled by the tyranny of profit maximization, many of these people become rabidly opportunistic, vengeful, distrustful, and calculating. It is sad not only because of the waste of human potential, but even more because of the unhappiness the resulting impoverishment causes in these people.

The system we advocate, management by missions (MBM), which we shall explain in the following chapters, is not a complete departure from MBO. It involves refocusing the MBO system to give each person's work a clear purpose. The ultimate goal of management by missions is to ensure that, regardless of rewards or punishments, the company's members work with a sense of mission.

5

What is a company's mission?

The concept of mission has been current in the world of business for more than half a century. In 1943, R.W. Johnson wrote the Johnson & Johnson (J&J) "Credo," which has survived to this day. A similar exercise was carried out in 1962 by Tom Watson, son of the founder of IBM, when he wrote the company's "Basic Beliefs."

In J&J, 40 years after the drafting of the "Credo," the then CEO Jim Burke claimed to spend nearly 40 percent of his time promoting those principles among the organization's members. Nowadays, as a statement of the company's responsibilities to customers, employees, managers, community, and shareholders, the J&J "Credo" remains in force and the company makes numerous efforts to strengthen and perpetuate that legacy.

In IBM, in the 1990s, when Louis V. Gerstner took over as CEO, the founding principles still exerted a powerful influence on the culture of the company as a whole. Gerstner himself made great efforts to update Watson's "Basic Beliefs" and adapt them to the company's new situation and environment.

Gradually, over the second half of the twentieth century, the idea of the corporate mission took root in companies. Its period of greatest popularity, especially in North America and parts of Europe, was the late 1980s and early 1990s, driven by the rise of cultural theories in the early 1980s. A study carried out by Bain & Co. and The Planning Forum in 1994 shows how important the mission had become by the mid-1990s. In interviews with more than 500 managers, the researchers analyzed 25 different management tools, including performance-related pay, workplace climate surveys, total quality, reengineering, customer satisfaction surveys, and so on. Based on the results of these interviews, they identified the mission as the most highly valued management tool, used in 90 percent of the companies in the sample.[1]

Since then, the mission continues to be acknowledged as a high-value-added management practice. The vast majority of *Fortune* 500 companies, and practically all those classified among the 100 Best Companies to Work For, have some kind of mission statement. In summary, the mission has been a fact of management life for close to half a century and is today one of the main management tools used by companies around the world.

Mission and "sense of mission"

The enduring popularity is sure to confound those who think that the mission is more of a fad, or simply a marketing ploy. And they are not always wrong. In many of the companies we studied, we found that the mission genuinely adds value. We also found, however, that for some companies it is just a bit of razzmatazz. Often it boils down to much ado about nothing: a period of reflection, followed by a great public fanfare, without any real consistency. This disappointing outcome – what might be described as "mission failure" – is something we shall come back to in more detail later on. The main point is that there is a big difference between simply defining a mission and creating a real sense of mission in the company.[2]

This type of pointless exercise affects other processes apart from the mission. Many companies have obtained similarly disappointing results in total quality, reengineering, or competency systems. If you take total quality systems, for example, there is a big difference between having a quality certificate and actually achieving high quality in all areas of the company.

To understand the mission's potential as a management tool, we need to ask ourselves, to what extent are we capable of building a sense of mission at work? In the 1950s, Peter Drucker[3] insisted that people's sense of mission can operate on different levels. To illustrate, he told the tale of three men who worked cutting large blocks of stone. When asked what they were doing, the first man replied, "I'm earning a living." The second, without stopping his work, said, "I'm doing the best job of stone-cutting in the whole country." The third stopped for a moment, looked up, and said, "I'm building a cathedral." A manager who focuses exclusively on the function, task, or goal may see three people doing the same job. But anyone who knows what it really means to manage a company knows very well the difference between "stonecutting" and "building a cathedral."

Theoretically speaking, this issue has been discussed in the literature on motivation in companies. Every person has the potential to be moved by three types of motives[4] (Figure 5.1): extrinsic motives (what the person receives "in exchange" for his work); intrinsic motives (the pleasure or learning he gets out of his work); and transcendent motives (what others get out of his work).

It is easy enough to find people who have not developed this potential in a balanced way. And yet,

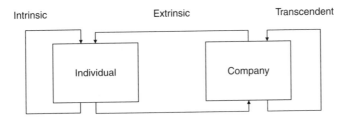

Figure 5.1 Types of motives

even these people secretly want to know what they are working for, and are pleased when they find that their work is of some good to somebody. In fact, this is the essence of the sense of mission. It is up to the leader to foster and continually draw attention to the transcendent meaning of the work each person does.

In the course of our research and consulting work we have found that people are eager to find a sense of mission in their daily work. To illustrate, the following are two opinions that we have heard quite regularly from middle managers and employees in different companies:

> It is essential that the company have a definite mission and that all the employees know what it is. The mission must be acceptable and achievable. It mustn't be a label, part of the corporate image, but a genuine performance driver, the glue that holds the company's members together.

> In this company, the only way to set clear objectives for all the people who work here is by having a mission. Having a clearly communicated mission fosters motivation and commitment among the entire workforce.

These and other similar expressions, which might have been taken from a Christmas speech or the chairman's letterhead, are spontaneous remarks that we have gathered from hundreds of people. This suggests to us that transcendent motivation at work is not just a theory.

As we said earlier, the need to contribute, to give meaning to daily work, is not exclusive to visionary chairmen or exceptionally committed managers. As Professor Simons[5] of Harvard Business School says,

> We all have a deep-seated need to contribute- to devote time and energy to worthwhile endeavors. But companies often make it difficult for employees to understand the larger purpose of their efforts or to see how they can add value in a way that can make a difference. Individuals want to understand the organization's purpose and how they can contribute, but senior managers must unleash this potential.

How to create a sense of mission: content, credibility, and urgency

Creating a sense of mission throughout the company requires more than simply writing the mission down on a piece of paper. In our experience, the mission must satisfy three basic conditions: content, credibility, and urgency. These three characteristics reinforce one another in building a sense of mission, so if any one of them fails, the sense of mission will suffer.

Content

A contentful mission is a contribution that makes people proud to do what they do. The mission content may vary in breadth, depth, and richness. For example, if a company's mission is to maximize profit for shareholders and nothing else, employees are unlikely to identify with it (unless they happen also to be shareholders). Thus, with a low-content mission, the sense of mission dwindles (and may even disappear completely). This is one reason why most companies give their mission more content, so that it expresses their commitment to the various stakeholders (employees, customers, shareholders, local community, etc.).

Credibility

A high-content mission can serve no useful purpose without credibility. In fact, that is the problem with many companies and managers: they lack credibility. On the one hand, you have a deep mission and rich values; on the other, a management system that assesses and rewards people based on increasingly aggressive economic objectives, which sometimes even run counter to the mission. This inconsistency cannot be resolved (and is more likely to be exacerbated) by internal propaganda or Christmas speeches by the general manager about the importance of the mission. The mission is what the company does, not what it would like to do, or what people think is "politically correct." When we define a mission, we must make sure that we are not talking about something different from what the company actually does, and that the company's management systems are truly aligned with that mission.

Credibility depends not only on the management system, but also on the role of the leader. The leader must therefore satisfy two requirements: (1) he must set an example of commitment to the mission; and (2) he must generate trust among his immediate subordinates (what is commonly known as earning people's trust).

Urgency

If there is no urgency to achieve something, it is because there is no real sense of mission. A team or organization that does not have urgent and demanding goals has succumbed to paternalism, understood as a disease of unity. Competent companies are never content with what they have achieved to date; their sense of mission always demands more. Good leaders are demanding, and very good leaders are very demanding. But they are also realists. A manager who sets unattainable goals is not a good leader, but a despot. Making "realistic demands" requires a balance based on a thorough knowledge of the market, people's abilities, and available technology.

Urgency is not the same as stress. In fact, the two have completely opposite effects. Urgency leads to action, intense effort, and focused decisions. Stress, by contrast, leads to paralysis, incapacity for sustained effort, and dispersion. Stress is caused by irrational external pressure which the subject cannot control. In fact, a bad leader amplifies stress. If we could take a snapshot of stress in an organization, it would be easy to detect bad leaders because when they are under pressure from above, instead of converting that pressure into urgency via a sense of mission, all they do is amplify the stress and transmit it to their subordinates. Unlike stress, urgency comes from within, because a thing is worth doing or needs to be done; always out of personal conviction. A good leader is one who knows how to instill in his subordinates a healthy sense of urgency in the service of a mission.

To achieve this, the mission must be embodied in demanding and realistic objectives that maintain a high level of urgency. A mission must be aimed at ambitious and attainable results. Otherwise, it is a dead mission that will induce cynicism throughout the organization.

Therefore, to create a sense of mission a company must have a content-rich mission that is credible to all members and that is put into practice with a sense of urgency. Now that we have defined the criteria for assessing a company's capacity to create a sense of mission, we must consider how to correctly define a mission.

Mission definition

Since the 1960s, the word "mission" has had different interpretations and emphases in academic circles and in business. Sometimes, there has been confusion between the mission and other things such as vision, strategic objectives, corporate philosophy, corporate principles, and so on. On conducting a brief historical review, we turn up a variety of definitions, most of them complementary to one another.

Drucker, P., 1974:[6]

- What our business is and what it should be?

- The company's no. 1 objective.

Clark, R., 1986:[7]

- The product offered.

- The technology used.

- The market the company serves.

Muckian and Arnold, 1989:[8]

- Who are we?

- What are we trying to do?

- Who do we serve?

- What or who determines our success?

Campbell and Nash 1992:[9]

- Strategy.

- The company's values.

- Policies and standards of behavior.

Senge, P. 1998:[10]

- Company's reason of being.

- What the organization is for?

- What the company contributes?

Faced with such variety, the first question is how to establish a definition of the mission that is consistent with the integral model presented previously. Not just any mission definition will do. In fact, some companies' missions, as they define them, are not, strictly speaking, missions.

In this book we define the mission as "The contribution that characterizes a group or an organization's identity."[11]

For example, a company's mission must be the contribution that characterizes that company's identity, just as the mission of a team must be the contribution that characterizes the team's identity.

Some supposed corporate "missions" do not fit this description; for example, any mission described in positional terms to be number one in a particular industry, or the industry benchmark or best in class, or one of the top 20 in a particular ranking, and so on. These may be more or less realistic objectives that may help a company fulfill its mission, but they are not the mission as such.[12] The mission is the contribution that can give meaning to such goals: why do we want to be number one in this industry?

The mission is a contribution, not a position; and a contribution is primarily a service, a specific way of solving real problems affecting individuals, groups, or society as a whole. But not just any contribution is a mission. A mission is a contribution that defines a company's identity, that gives a particular company, department, team, or worker a reason for existence. For example, donating 1 percent of the company's profits to charity may be an important contribution, but it is very unlikely to be the company's defining contribution, so it cannot be the company's mission (though it may still be a valuable contribution that is consistent with the company's values and so is worth maintaining).

Our analysis of more than 1300 mission statements from around the world confirms that the great majority of companies agree with our definition of what constitutes a mission. Many of them specifically use the term "mission." Others give it a different name: "corporate principles," "organizational purpose," "corporate philosophy," "credo," "corporate objectives," and so on. Whatever the case, it is fair to say that widespread company practice endorses the definition we have given. And in most cases, the definition may be applied without any major change in the way the company formulates its mission.

Nevertheless, given that the mission presents itself in such a variety of guises, we shall make a distinction between the mission in the strict sense and the mission in the broad sense.

In the strict sense, the mission is centered exclusively on "the contribution" that defines a group or an organization's identity. In the broad sense, the mission not only includes that contribution, but also comprises other related aspects, such as values, social responsibility, ethical principles, corporate policies, and so on.

For example, in a worldwide car manufacturer well known company, mission statement was defined using the "mission" in the strict sense of the term, while its values came under a different heading.

> Our mission is to continuously improve our products and services so as to satisfy our customers' needs, allowing us to prosper as a business and provide a reasonable return for our shareholders, the owners of the business.

The mission of Mondragón Corporación Cooperativa (MCC) is a mission in the broad sense, in that it covers various aspects relating to the nature and history of the company, as well as its foundational values:

> Mondragón Corporación Cooperativa (MCC) is a socioeconomic business organization with deep cultural roots in the Basque Country. It was created by and for people and is modeled on the basic principles of our Cooperative Experience. It is committed to the environment, competitiveness and customer satisfaction, with the aim of generating wealth in society through business development and job creation, preferably on a cooperative basis. MCC:
>
> ■ Is founded on a commitment to solidarity and employs democratic methods in its organization and management.
>
> ■ Encourages employee participation and involvement in the management, results and ownership of its companies, which pursue a common initiative aimed at harmonizing social, business and personal progress.

▪ Promotes training and innovation by developing human and technological capabilities, and uses a specific management model to attain leadership positions and foster cooperation.

(Mondragón Corporación Cooperativa:
Mission statement)

The stakeholder model

Many companies have adopted the stakeholder concept[13] and have incorporated it in their mission. To know what is the contribution that defines their identity, they diagnose the needs of the company's main stakeholders: customers, shareholders, employees, and so on.

Customers

Of the 1300 company missions we have analyzed, few fail to mention the customer in one way or another. Nowadays, it is difficult to conceive of a content-rich mission that does not include the company's contribution to customers as a fundamental ingredient.

The company's contribution to its customers may be expressed in various ways. Companies in very different industries may describe it in similar terms, while others in the same industry, even in the same business, may see it very differently.

Shareholders

Traditionally, companies' contribution to shareholders has been taken to consist of two things: payment of dividends and increases in the company's value. These two things are what is today understood as value creation. Briefly, value creation consists of providing remuneration, in the form of dividends or capital gains, above the cost of capital. Many companies' mission statements use terms such as "fair remuneration," "return," "profit," "value," or "value creation."

Yet value creation is not necessarily companies' only contribution to their shareholders. Management transparency and good corporate governance are examples of mission contents that go beyond the purely financial dimension. Such things may be particularly important in the case of family businesses or cooperatives – as with Mondragón, for example.

Employees

There is a growing belief that companies have an obligation toward those who allow them to exist: people.

Richard Branson – the hugely successful entrepreneur who founded Virgin Records, Virgin Atlantic Airways, and many other companies – has said in numerous speeches that in Virgin Atlantic people come first, customers second, and shareholders third.[14]

Authors such as Pfeffer[15] have demonstrated, with numbers and real-world examples, that the best strategy for any company is to "put people first." This motto is preached by many companies that have made contribution to people one of the main pillars of their mission.

These three stakeholders – customers, shareholders, and employees – are what many companies and authors describe as key stakeholders or "primary constituencies."[16] They are the base on which most company missions around the world are founded.

Other stakeholders

Besides the primary constituencies, many missions mention other stakeholders, such as suppliers, competitors, society at large, the public authorities, political associations, and so on.

In our opinion, a mission should be centered on the stakeholders to whom the company has a special obligation to contribute. And it should state clearly and specifically the nature of each contribution.

An example of a mission based on the company's commitments to its stakeholders is the one developed by the oil company Repsol YPF:

1. *Commitment to shareholders*: To offer our shareholders sustained value creation, guaranteeing transparency in management, and good corporate governance.

2. *Commitment to our customers*: To fully satisfy our customers' expectations, making an effort to anticipate and be aware of their needs.

3. *Commitment to our partners and suppliers*: To build relationships with partners and suppliers founded on reciprocal contribution and mutual respect, and above all, based on trust, and product and service quality.

4. *Commitment to employees*: To attract, motivate, and retain the best professionals, offering them an attractive place to work. To guarantee and promote professional development opportunities with a world-class employer. Career development will be based on OBJECTIVE assessment of professional merit, within a framework of nondiscrimination, so that people are proud to be part of our organization.

5. *Commitment to society*: To contribute to sustainable development of the society we live in, and to assume a firm commitment to support the communities in which we do business. Care for the environment, environmental safety, and commitment, and respect for human rights are part of our strategy and ensure that our businesses grow in a way that is compatible with the principles of sustainable development.

Actually defining the mission

We cannot end this chapter without considering exactly how a company should go about defining its mission. Some authors and consultants have tried to draw up mission definition manuals or specify standard processes.[17] We believe, however, that such exercises have more risks than advantages. For example, a particular process may be very effective in a listed company but not in a family firm.

Nonetheless, the following suggestions may be helpful for defining the mission:

1. An important decision, before defining the mission, is who should be involved in the process. Every organization will have to find its own answer to that question. It is common practice, however, to involve a fair number of members of the organization. If people have had a say in defining the mission, the result will be more robust and people will be more likely to take ownership of the mission and identify with it. In some cases, the company may also involve people belonging to other interest groups, such as customers, consumers, unions, or suppliers.

2. It is important that the mission be easy to communicate and get across to people. A 20-page exposition may be a laudable theoretical exercise, but it will be difficult to put across to the organization as a whole. A company's mission must be concise, broad in content, and expressed in rather general terms, so as to accommodate everything the organization does and foster lateral thinking.

3. Another vital consideration is how to win the approval of the company's governing bodies. Although the task of defining the mission may

sometimes be delegated to a mixed work team (management and nonmanagement staff), the mission will have to be approved by those who govern the company.

4. Lastly, another much debated issue is whether the company's mission should be reviewed at regular intervals or not. There are those who say that a mission should not be changed unless there are serious reasons for doing so, such as a merger or divestment. And even then, they argue, the mission should not be changed any more than strictly necessary. Others, in contrast, prefer to think of the mission as not being "written on stone." They contend that it should be reviewed and updated every two or three years. Among the various company missions we analyzed, we found that there is a tendency for the company's mission to be reviewed at long intervals of five to ten years, or in exceptional circumstances.

As we said earlier, the mission in the broad sense includes criteria for choosing the means to realize the mission's contribution. These criteria may be presented in various ways, but traditionally they are expressed in the form of values. In the next chapter we shall explain what values are and how they can help create a balanced culture.

6

The values of a balanced culture

Mission and values are intimately related. A company committed to a particular mission may develop very different cultures, depending on the values it actually lives by. For instance, if a company assumes a commitment to satisfy customers' needs and defines its values as profitability and ethicality, that commitment will likely translate as "satisfy customers' needs ethically and profitably." Evidence of the connection is the fact that companies usually present their mission and values together. That is no coincidence. Often, a company's mission can only be fully understood in light of its values.

Mission and values are a whole, on which the company's culture is founded. If the mission is the purpose that guides action, values are the criteria that guide the decision as to the most appropriate course in any given situation. Values tell us *how* we must accomplish our mission. A mission can be accomplished in many different ways. The only requirement is that the values effectively serve the mission.

Choosing the right values – values that are consistent with the mission – is an important part of what we have called "intrategy."

Thus, mission and values can be seen as being encompassed within the concept of the mission in the broad sense described in the previous chapter. From now on, we shall use the following definition of the mission in the broad sense: "the contribution and values that define a group or an organization's identity."

Where values come from

Rarely do managers describe their companies without mentioning the organization's values: passion for a job well done, innovation, customer service, perseverance, rigorous pursuit of excellence, quality, desire for improvement, ethics, and so on.

Salvador García and Simón Dolan, specialists in organizational psychology, define three dimensions of the term "value":[1]

- *Ethical-strategic dimension*: This is the understanding that one type of action is better than another for achieving certain purposes or goals. Such values include quality (as opposed to shoddy workmanship), team work (as opposed to individualism), or ethics (as opposed to fraud).

- *Economic dimension*: This is the scope or significance of the importance of people, objects, ideas, actions, feelings, or facts. Such values include innovation, creativity, or trust.

- *Psychological dimension*: This is the moral quality that moves a person to resolutely undertake major ventures and courageously face the dangers (we could also define it as absence of fear). In this dimension, the value is the courage of an individual or group of individuals.

Not wishing to be drawn into a lengthy psychological digression – among other things, because this is a book about management, not about psychology – from now on the term "value" will be used here to refer to the first two dimensions.

Values are formed through *interpreting* reality. As shown in Figure 6.1, any such interpretation is based on two things: beliefs and perceptions.

First, values are based on beliefs, that is, the models we have about the importance of certain behaviors. What I think is important is a value for me. For instance, the belief that "working together in a coordinated way and sharing information is good for employees and good for the company as a whole"

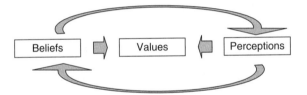

Figure 6.1 Where values come from

may make "team work" a value. As beliefs evolve and change, so do values.

Secondly, perceptions exert a powerful influence on values. For example, if we work in a company in which innovation is a habitual behavior, we are very likely to accept innovation as a value. Similarly, what we see as a value for people around us may become a value for us too. That is apparent in trends such as total quality or the growing concern for the environment. For example, if we perceive that quality is valued by most members of an organization, we will not be surprised to find quality present as a value in our own activities, too. Of course, the same reasoning also applies in reverse.

Ultimately, we can say that beliefs influence perceptions, and vice versa. For example, if a manager believes that one of his subordinates is incompetent, that will naturally affect the manager's perceptions. He will tend to focus more on what the subordinate does wrong than on what he does right. Furthermore, focusing exclusively on the subordinate's mistakes will reinforce the manager's belief that the subordinate is indeed incompetent.

Thanks to this effect, whereby perceptions and beliefs reinforce one another, people's values tend to be stable. This explanation of the origin of values may help us to understand other aspects of the cultural dynamic in organizations, such as why there is a natural resistance to change, or why it is so difficult to introduce new values into an organization.

Defining an organization's values

In most organizations, especially in very successful ones, there are certain values that have stayed with people for many years. To some extent, those values make up the organization's culture. By values we mean specific criteria or ways of interpreting reality which, over time, become a "way of being and doing things." As a rule, it does not take many values to define a culture: three or four are enough, certainly no more than seven or eight. This is because when we talk about a company's values, we are referring to the highest values, the ones thought to have "exceptional value," the ones most closely related to the company's core identity. These values must be deeply rooted in members' beliefs. They must also be reinforced by the way the company does business day to day.

Ericsson describes its core values as follows:

> Professionalism, respect and perseverance are the values that are the foundation of the Ericsson culture, guiding us in our daily work – how we relate to people and how we do business.
>
> (Ericsson, Core Values)

However, we must ask ourselves how realistic and how appropriate such values statements are to the company's needs. Many companies' real values are quite unlike the ones cited in their public announcements.

In other words, what must a company's values be like in order to have a real impact on its culture?

Given that values are based on people's beliefs and perceptions, there is no such thing as values in the abstract. Strictly speaking, values are always values for somebody. In this sense, values are different from other aspects of the company, such as strategy. The members of a company may more or less agree with the strategy, and the strategy may be more or less popular; but once the strategy has been decided and agreed, it is valid for the whole company. The same cannot be said of values. Values cannot be defined "from outside" the world of the people in the organization. An organization's values will only be effective if they are accepted as values by the organization's members. That is why, if we want to define the values of an organization, we must first understand the underlying values: the perceptions and beliefs of the organization's members.

We cannot hope to understand an organization's underlying values merely by reading the values statement drawn up by top management. We must ask a representative sample of organizational members at least the following two questions:

1. What are the most characteristic values of the organization as it is now? (Perceptions)

2. What values do you think the company should have in order to succeed? (Beliefs)

Once we know the underlying values, assuming the mission has been defined, we can draw up a reliable values statement. For a company's values statement to be reliable, the values must meet three conditions related to the mission criteria of content, credibility, and urgency. The three conditions are as follows:

1. The company's values must be in the service of the company's mission. They must be consistent with the mission; that is, they must serve the mission. Values tell us how the mission must be fulfilled. That is why we cannot specify the values until we have defined the mission. If, for whatever reason, the mission changes, we will have to decide whether the values are still valid or not.

2. They must be deeply held by the organization's members: they must be present at least in their perceptions or beliefs. It is no use defining a set of values that do not engage the company's members or that are valid for only a few. Ideally, a company's values will be perceived and believed as such by the company's members.

3. They must be reflected in the company's day-to-day operations and management systems. There must be consistency between what the company preaches and what it practices day to day. Espousal of a company's values must be demanded with a sense of responsibility and good example. Values are for action.

This latter condition is illustrated by Cadbury Schweppes' values statement, which ends as follows:

> Cadbury Schweppes' commitment to the values I have expounded will not be judged by this written statement, but by our actions. (. . .) Pride in what we do at work is important for each one of us; it encourages us give the best of ourselves; [T]hat is the hallmark of a successful company. To the extent that we put the beliefs stated here into action, we may be deserving of that pride.
>
> (Cadbury Schweppes: Corporate statement)[2]

How values change and evolve

Over time, some values change and evolve. Some fall into the background, while others come to the fore. People may be affected by a new strategic focus, the way a manager behaves, or changes in the company's environment. Current values may be called into question or new ones brought to prominence by a change of beliefs or perceptions.

At one stage, a company may set its sights on geographical expansion. At some later stage, it may prefer to reorganize or consolidate. In many cases, the same value may be reinterpreted so as to acquire a new meaning. In the 1970s, quality was a value associated with products. Today, it is understood as something that concerns all the processes and activities of a company.

However, changes in values must not prevent a company from maintaining certain "key values" over time. Collins and Porras[3] suggest that one of the things that make "visionary" companies so successful is the fact of having maintained a set of values for decades. For many companies, values are one of their main advantages against competitors. It can be relatively easy to copy a product, strategy, technological innovation, or production method; but developing a set of values in a company can take years.

Values are one of the key success factors in business; yet they can also be a cause of failure. Not having certain values, or acquiring the wrong values – the kind that block a company's strategic development – can be an overwhelming competitive disadvantage in the short to medium term. It is not uncommon for companies to find themselves outclassed by their rivals precisely because they lack the "human capital" to implement certain strategies.

On one occasion, the European vice president of an electronics company described us the scope of this problem. Although he knew the strategies for success in his industry, he had found it impossible to implement them in his company. In his opinion, the problem boiled down to the fact that people did not want to excel: "We owe the great achievements of our past to our desire to excel. But that value has not remained alive in our people. We have grown used to things' running themselves, and whenever we need bold changes, we feel incapable of carrying them out."

Balanced values

As we have seen, it is very difficult to give any general rules about how values should be developed in a company. Every organization will develop a particular set of values, depending on factors such as its history, the industry in which it operates, the philosophy of its founders or managers, and so on.

Nevertheless, to find out whether there is any common pattern in the values of different companies, we analyzed 48 companies of different nationalities and obtained a total of 266 values. Based on our results, we classified the values as follows:[4]

1. *Business values*: Values relating to the company's business and profit-making activity. Examples include perseverance, efficiency, professionalism or results orientation.

2. *Relational values*: Values that foster quality in interpersonal relations. They include, for example, communication, team work or respect for people.

3. *Development values*: Values aimed at differentiating and continuously improving the company. Examples include innovation, creativity, learning or continuous improvement.

4. *Contribution values*: Values aimed at doing more for stakeholders than strictly required by the business relationship. They include, for example, customer satisfaction, interest in people, social responsibility.

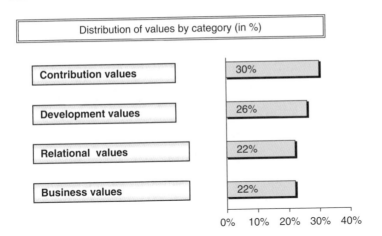

Figure 6.2   Distribution of values by category

Figure 6.2 shows how the values held by the companies in our sample are distributed among these four categories.

The results suggest that in what we might call a "healthy corporate culture" the four categories – business, relational, development and contribution – carry roughly equal weight. Interviews with a large number of managers confirm this principle of balance: a culturally healthy company must cultivate and develop values in all four cultural categories. This requirement for balance may serve as a guide for companies in their choice of values. A practical suggestion would be to choose one or two values in each category. Seriously neglecting any one dimension may generate a dysfunctional culture.

Apart from choosing the right values, we also need to ensure they are properly implemented throughout the company, making whatever changes may be necessary to achieve a balanced culture. In our research, we found companies with clearly dysfunctional cultures. Although they had defined and officially promoted a set of "key values" in all four cultural categories, those key values had never "taken" in the organization. In most of these companies, the real culture was centered almost exclusively on business values. Because of this imbalance, values such as team work, innovation, or customer service came to the bottom of the list and were seen as empty words rather than as a fact of daily life in the company.

Cultural change management

Developing values and managing cultural change are two of the most difficult tasks for managers. On the one hand, companies must preserve and strengthen the values that make them successful. On the other, they must detect any deficiencies or negative values and formulate action plans to remedy them.

There are no clear methods for managing cultural change. One of the earliest methods (one that has many adherents) is that of the early 1980s best-seller *Corporate Cultures*, by Terrence Deal and Allen Kennedy.[5] The authors define seven ingredients of cultural change as follows:

1. Appoint a hero to lead the process (a change sponsor, someone in the organization who is respected and has charisma).

2. Identify an external threat that stimulates change (the better it is understood within the company, the more likely the change will succeed).

3. Perform transition rituals as central change elements (getting people involved through focus groups, dinners, trips, or other types of corporate events).

4. Conduct intense training and communication about the new values and behavior patterns (brochures, video clips, etc).

5. Bring in outside consultants (charismatic conflict management experts to encourage people to change).

6. Give tangible signs of the new direction (organizational changes, promotions, etc.).

7. Insist on the importance of employment security during the transition (show confidence about job stability and, if layoffs are necessary, establish a clear and objective policy that removes any doubt in the minds of those left behind).

The influence of Deal and Kennedy's proposals is apparent in many handbooks and theories about implementing cultural change in companies. Some of their "ingredients" have taken new forms and names, but essentially they remain the same. However, these tools cannot bring about lasting cultural change by themselves (though they may be useful for promoting and driving change).

The basic problem is that, except in very rare cases, they never become part of the management system. It comes down to the fact that it is very difficult to get people to accept and practice something that the management system does not assess or require. After all these years struggling to establish missions and values, many companies admit they have not succeeded. This is what we call "mission failure."

Part III

Toward a New Management Model

7

The mission chart

As we have seen, a company's mission is a general statement that distills the essence of the contribution that defines the company's identity. This statement is unspecific by definition and not directly applicable to any particular context. There is nothing wrong with that. What would be wrong would be to imagine that a mission, so defined, is sufficient to guide decision making throughout the organization. In fact, strictly speaking, a company's mission has no particular meaning for the organization's members. What does have a meaning, though, is how each person can contribute to the accomplishment of that mission. For that, we need to clarify what "contributing to the accomplishment of the mission" means for each job.

Also, as we move down the organization chart, the level of identification with the company's mission may diminish. The main reason, in most cases, is that companies' efforts to put the mission across to their members often are confined to repeating a particular catchphrase or set of rather general statements. In our view, this is totally inadequate. Despite the amount of management effort and time devoted to communication, the mission tends to be regarded with detachment and skepticism.

The challenge is to bring the mission to life for employees at all levels, so that it does not remain at the level of general statements. Because a company's mission is accomplished through the combined efforts of all its members, this relationship needs to be spelled out at the individual level. The best way to communicate a mission is to make every member of the organization aware of exactly how he contributes to mission fulfillment. We therefore suggest that the mission be systematically deployed to the company's various departments, teams, and, eventually, people.

We have created a management tool, called "shared missions," to achieve this purpose and bring the mission into the everyday practice of the company's individual jobs and functions. Shared missions are mission deployments to different departments and levels of the organization. To complement the shared missions we have the interdependency matrix, which shows how different areas cooperate to fulfill the company's mission. Lastly, for the mission to be deployed effectively, it needs to be translated into specific measurement indicators.

Shared missions

A shared mission is an area of responsibility whose purpose is to help accomplish the higher-level mission. Just as the company's mission is the reason why the company exists, the shared mission is the reason why each of the company's units, departments, and functional areas exists. Thus, just as the company's mission is the contribution that defines the company's identity, the shared mission of an area or department is the contribution that defines the area's or the department's identity. Similarly, like the overall mission, each shared mission must have content, credibility, and urgency.

In other words, it must share in the higher-level mission (hence the term "shared mission"). Sharing means participating, taking responsibility for something that is part of a whole. For example, a team member's mission will be aimed at accomplishing the team mission. That way, everybody shares, one way or another, in the corporate mission. What's more, the lower-level missions, together, must accomplish the higher-level mission. The missions would not be complete if accomplishing all the lower-level missions did not entail accomplishing the higher-level mission.

In practice, defining the shared mission of an area or department requires careful thought and analysis. In most cases, we have found that existing organizational information (job descriptions, organization charts, process designs, etc.) is inadequate for this purpose. It tends to be about *what we do* and does not even address the core of any shared mission, namely, *what we do it for*. The main purpose of shared missions is to fill this vacuum, both in operational roles (production, logistics, sales, etc.) and in staff or support functions (finance, administration, human resources, etc.).

In order to define the shared mission of both operational and support functions in a given area or department, we need to investigate how this area or department helps to accomplish the corporate mission. This investigation will vary according to each company's individual mission. As a rule, it will cover issues such as how each area contributes to customers, employees, shareholders, suppliers, even society at large (especially in organizations with a pronouncedly social mission).

To some extent, the shared mission changes the way members of an area or department understand their identity and their contribution to the company as a whole. For example, very often shared missions make it clear to employees that customer service is a matter for the whole company, not just certain areas or departments. The same goes for employee development: shared missions bring home the fact that employee development is not the exclusive responsibility of any one area or function but is shared by all areas and levels of the company.

On the other hand, there is no such thing, in our model, as an "anonymous" mission in the sense of a mission without an owner. Every mission *belongs* to someone. For example, a company's mission belongs to its general manager. A department's shared mission belongs to the head of department.

Whoever has responsibility for a mission is the mission's *owner*. Those who help to accomplish the mission are mission *participants*. For example, the owner of the sales department's mission is the sales director, and his subordinates are participants in that mission. Besides his specific mission, every manager also has a *managerial mission:*[1] to contribute to his subordinates' development. A manager must therefore have the necessary aptitudes to accomplish both his specific mission and his managerial mission.

As a structured, joint exercise, defining shared missions is the first step in the cultural change that is the goal of management by missions. Each area or department is no longer concerned exclusively with the "what" or the "how." Its focus is broadened and deepened to encompass the "why," or the "what for." This brings the company's mission to life within the scope of the different functions.

Criteria for defining a shared mission

To be properly defined, shared missions must satisfy three fundamental criteria.

Criterion of inclusion

Inclusion means that each shared mission must contribute to the accomplishment of the next higher-level mission and, ultimately, the corporate mission. If this criterion is not met, there is a risk that individual areas or departments will establish missions that diverge from the corporate mission. To define a shared mission, we must take the higher-level mission as our reference point and ask ourselves, How does my area or department contribute to achieve the higher-level mission?

For example, if the corporate mission is oriented toward customer satisfaction, employee development, and a fair shareholder return, then each area will have to ask itself, How does our area contribute to customer satisfaction? How does it contribute to employee development? How does it contribute to providing a fair shareholder return?

Like the company's mission, the shared mission should not be defined in positional terms; nor should it merely list activities or responsibilities. In defining a shared mission, we are aiming to determine exactly how an activity contributes, how it adds value. For example, an internal audit department may put a lot of effort into gathering data and drafting reports; but that is not its shared mission. The question we must ask is, How do those reports help to fulfill the company's mission?

Criterion of complementarity

Complementarity ensures that there is a horizontal or process logic among the various shared missions. It is important to ensure that the shared missions adopted by the different areas or functions do not compete with one another. On the contrary, the shared missions at any given level should be complementary in every respect. Taking customer service as an example common to most companies' missions, management must see to it that each area defines its contribution to customers in a way that is complementary to the way other areas define theirs. The same applies to other mission contributions, such as the contribution to shareholders, employees, or suppliers.

In practice, the complementarity criterion means that shared missions tend to be defined from a process perspective. This way, each area is seen as a value-added generating unit, rather than merely as a performer of certain functions.

Criterion of consistency

Consistency ensures that the mission is deployed throughout the company in a coordinated way. While complementarity measures whether shared missions are consistent across the organization, consistency tells us whether each shared mission is aligned with its higher-level mission or missions.

In our experience, an effective way to ensure vertical consistency among missions is to deploy the mission from the top down, starting with the basic corporate mission statements and cascading them to lower levels. In practice, one way to guarantee deployment consistency is by requiring that each shared mission be approved by the owner of the higher-level mission. This way, top-management guidelines effectively reach the base of the organization, and the shared missions are aligned with the chain of command.

Table 7.1 Criteria a mission must meet

Criteria a mission must meet	
Corporate mission and shared missions	Content Credibility Urgency
Shared missions	Inclusion Complementarity Consistency

To sum up, the corporate mission and the shared missions must meet the criteria of content, credibility, and urgency. The shared missions in particular must also meet the criteria of inclusion, complementarity, and consistency (Table 7.1).

The interdependency matrix

One of the most important facts about companies is that people, activities, and departments are interdependent. How well each person does his job depends to a large extent on how well other people do theirs. Several prominent management thinkers of the 1980s pointed out that one of the errors of traditional management systems is "the common assumption that if each part or division (of an organization) does its bit, the company as a whole will achieve its ultimate goal. This is not generally true: the parts are almost always interdependent."[2]

The same applies to the process of deploying the mission in shared missions. It is not enough merely to define how each area contributes to the completion of the company's mission (direct contribution). We also need to identify how the different areas must cooperate with one another in order to fulfill the overall mission (indirect contribution). This is what defines the interdependency relationships between areas or departments.

The complete set of interdependency relationships constitutes what we call the "interdependency matrix." The interdependency matrix shows the internal customer–supplier relationships within a company. It is generally not all that difficult to identify the interdependency relationships between areas or departments. In practice, we need to ask ourselves, What contributions do I need from other areas (internal suppliers) in order to accomplish my shared mission? And what contributions do other areas (internal customers) need from me in order to accomplish their shared mission? Normally, company members are well aware of these relationships. The difficult thing is to design a really efficient (nonbureaucratic) interdependency matrix. This requires a full understanding of the company's internal processes and a mission-guided approach that takes all aspects of the company into account.

In all the companies we have worked with, constructing the interdependency matrix has brought huge improvements in cooperation between areas. This is because shared missions give cooperation a new purpose by orienting it toward a higher end. Constructing the interdependency matrix is therefore not just a technical exercise but helps to clarify the reasons to cooperate, inviting people to cooperate "out of a sense of mission." For example, we have found that after implementing the interdependency matrix, many departments rethink the way they cooperate with other areas and set new targets for "internal service."

In many cases, the benefits of the interdependency matrix, in terms of enhanced cooperation, have far surpassed expectations. We have taken this to some extent as proof that cooperating "out of a sense of mission" is much better than cooperating for other reasons (such as for purely financial rewards or other recompense). For our part, we have come to the conclusion that the lack of cooperation that drags so many organizations down is not a question of aptitude but of motives (or reasons) to cooperate. Thus, the interdependency matrix, linked to shared missions, offers a new perspective that can motivate people to cooperate in a structured and systematic way. This new form of cooperation is one of the main benefits of management by missions.

The mission chart

Together, the shared missions and the interdependency matrix make up what we call "the mission chart." The mission chart enriches and complements the traditional organization chart, with its hierarchy of relationships and functions, by giving each area or department a sense of mission.

The key to implementing the mission chart is to organize the company's departments and functions according to how they add value in the pursuit of the corporate mission. The difficult thing, though, is to design a really efficient organization. A mission that is not grounded in the company's internal processes, or an inefficient interdependency matrix, may be fruitless and impracticable.

These challenges may be met using techniques and tools familiar to those acquainted with process reengineering, such as process maps or value analysis.[3] However, there is a crucial difference between many reengineering practices and a mission chart. A mission chart does not aim exclusively for economic efficiency, but for efficiency in the "mission value chain." The mission value chain shows how each of the company's activities and functions relates to the contributions that the company's mission requires. That is why implementing the mission chart may entail a certain amount of organizational change, especially where functions or activities are duplicated, add no value, or are uncoupled from the logic of the processes that enable the company to accomplish its mission.

Specific values

Just as, at corporate level, the mission and values are integrated in the corporate purpose, the shared missions may in some cases be characterized by certain values, which we call "specific values." These specific values are complementary to the corporate values and apply to the owner and participants of a given shared mission. As a rule, it is best not to specify too many values. Between seven and ten, including corporate and specific values, will generally be enough.

Table 7.2 below shows a generic mission chart in which the company's mission is deployed through the sales, production, and finance departments. Each of these areas, in turn, defines one or two specific values, which complement the general corporate values.

The mission chart of a corporate group

Shared missions can also help solve the problems of identity resulting from mergers and acquisitions, which have been so common in recent decades. Subsidiaries very often find it difficult to formulate and specify their mission because they lack cohesive management or the necessary autonomy. This is the complaint voiced by the HR director of an insurance company that was taken over by an Italian multinational:

> Before, we had a clear corporate purpose. We knew who we were and what we were here for. Now, we have largely lost our identity. We lack a clear, shared mission. I'd even venture to suggest this is the main reason for the drop in productivity we've seen in recent years.

Several top managers of subsidiaries have asked us whether, in our opinion, a subsidiary has its

Table 7.2 Example of a mission chart

The mission chart

Company Corporate mission		Department		
	Sales	Production	Admin. & Finan.	Other depts.
Serve our customers	Exceed customers' expectations and needs	Satisfy customers' needs through quality and service	Optimize the financing of customer relations	…
Give shareholders a return on their capital	Ensure a profit margin on the company's products	Guarantee cost competitiveness	Monitor and analyze return on investment	…
Drive continuous improvement of our company	Translate customers' needs into proposals to improve products and processes	Implement improvements in products and processes	Provide the information needed to accomplish the company's mission	…
Promote staff well-being	Create a climate of professional growth, trust and recognition	Foster employee motivation and recognition	Foster employee autonomy and ongoing learning	…

Shared missions

Table 7.2 (Continued)

| | The mission chart | | | |
| | | **Department** | | |
Company **Corporate mission**	**Sales**	**Production**	**Admin. & Finan.**	**Other depts.**
Contribute to the community	Participate actively in social activities	Use resources rationally, respecting the environment	Comply with the law and ethical principles	...
Corporate values Unity Profitability Quality Fluid, sincere communication Creativity Training *Specific values*	Proactivity	Efficiency Planning	Transparency	...

own mission. We say, yes, it does, in every case. Subsidiaries must try to build and assert an identity of their own, consistent with their history and environment. Based on that identity, they must define their shared mission; that is, how they help to accomplish the mission of the group or holding company to which they belong.

An example of this is Abertis, a world leader in transport and communications infrastructure. Abertis uses a mission chart to deploy the group mission to the various business units (Motorways, Airports, Logistics, Car Parks, etc.). Thus, each business unit has its own shared mission, which is linked to the corporate mission through inclusion, complementarity, and consistency.

As globalization becomes the dominant economic model, the way a company deploys its mission to its subsidiaries or business units becomes increasingly complex and dependent on how the decision centers are organized. This makes it particularly important that the board and top management of large multinationals give subsidiary managers guidance on how to adapt the group mission to the particular environment and circumstances of their country, region, or industry.

The mission scorecard

Lastly, mission deployment would not be complete without the means to measure progress. Many managers, and management literature in general, would agree that measuring progress with indicators and ratios is essential for the day-to-day control of operations: "you can't manage what you can't measure."

To define indicators, we used the scorecard method, which we had been using before we started the MBM. And we have found that the existing methods, in particular Kaplan and Norton's balanced scorecard (BSC), are indeed a good starting point. However, there are certain important differences in outcome and procedure which we believe are worth briefly commenting on.

Scorecards came into use in the 1930s. They were based on ratios and indicators that recorded a company's principal management variables. In the 1990s, Kaplan and Norton gave an excellent critique of such scorecards. They pointed out that most of the indicators used by companies are essentially economic or financial, and short-term. By contrast, the BSC includes other indicators, based on a representation of cause–effect relationships which they called a "strategic map." Besides the financial perspective, the strategic map also encompasses the customer perspective, the process perspective, and the learning and growth perspective.

However, whenever we have tried to design scorecards based on the corporate mission, we have found that the BSC does not always cover every aspect of the mission. This is because the BSC uses the same preestablished perspectives for all companies, whereas a mission may include different perspectives. For this reason we regard the BSC as an intermediate solution.

Moreover, in the BSC approach, customer service, employee motivation, and community contribution are not ends in themselves, but means to improve a company's financial performance. With reference to quality enhancements or reduced customer response times, for example, Kaplan and Norton suggest that "Such improvements only benefit a company when they can be translated into improved sales, reduced operating expenses, or higher asset utilization."[4]

All these problems disappear when the scorecard is derived directly from the corporate mission and becomes a "mission scorecard" (MSC). The MSC is the result of translating the various mission statements into specific, measurable performance goals. One or more indicators are defined for each part of the company's mission. The mission scorecard thus derives directly from the corporate mission; it is not necessarily limited to financial indicators or preestablished areas or perspectives.

The main point of the MSC approach is that, ultimately, the only way to measure a company's success is in terms of mission completion. Anheuser–Busch's mission statement expresses this idea very clearly:

> (. . .) This mission statement provides a point of reference which we must use to assess the strategies of each of our businesses and measure their progress and results.
>
> (Anheuser–Busch, Mission statement)

Migrating from traditional scorecards or the BSC approach to the MSC approach is relatively easy. The MSC will usually include many of the indicators we use regularly in day-to-day management. In some cases, however, we will have to exercise our imagination and develop new indicators, especially for mission statements addressing intangibles such as employee satisfaction or impact on society. Once a mission scorecard is complete, it can be deployed throughout the company using shared missions at each level.

We can see an example of this in the information systems (IS) department of a large automotive OEM. Over the previous 5 years, the department had grown to serve more than 15 countries and had more than 50 employees. Realizing they were starting to struggle, management decided to reorganize. They began by defining the department's mission. With extensive employee participation, the IS department's mission was defined in terms of service to other areas of the company. IS being a support department, everybody agreed that the main mission was to serve other areas and contribute to the development of the organization's members.

Defining the mission was the first step; the second was to prepare the scorecard. Until then, the IS department had been using indicators that basically measured the development and implementation phase of computer applications. Many of these same indicators were used in the MSC, but they seemed inadequate to measure mission fulfillment. Accordingly, two new sections were added: a section on service and a section on staff training and development. Service indicators were obtained by soliciting feedback from other departments on the service they received from the IS department, and the usefulness of the new hardware and software implementations. For training, two new indicators were created: an effectiveness indicator and a perceived trainee satisfaction indicator. These indicators, together with those already in use, were used to bring about a transformation in the IS department so that its efforts were directed toward fuller, more effective completion of its mission: to serve other departments and to contribute to employee development and training. Figure 7.1 shows the department's scorecard. As we have seen, this scorecard is the fruit of serious thought about the mission and is designed to help accomplish that mission.

In addition to the benefits inherent in drawing up any kind of scorecard, the MSC has two crucial advantages. On the one hand, it makes it easier to manage intangibles; on the other, it makes the company's indicators more uniform and consistent

Service	2002 Actual	2003 Target	2003 Actual	Score
Satisfaction index (average assessment)	3.8	4.0	3.9	◯
System improvements (% of total proposed)	71	75	77	◯
Problem resolution (% of requests)	25	40	30	◯
Compliance with deadlines (% of total)	80	90	75	●

People	2002 Actual	2003 Target	2003 Actual	Score
Hours of training received (hours/dept. member)	18	50	40	◯
Hours of training given (hours/total users)	27	30	35	●
Assessment of training (scored from 1 to 5)	4.1	4.1	4.2	●
Effectiveness of training (% problems recurring)	40	30	34	◯

Hardware	2002 Actual	2003 Target	2003 Actual	Score
Server downtime (% of total)	1.4	1.3	1	◯
LAN downtime (% of total)	0.3	0.3	0.2	◯
WAN downtime (% of total)	1.9	1.5	2.3	●
Telecoms downtime (% of total)	0.8	0.6	0.7	◯

Software	2002 Actual	2003 Target	2003 Actual	Score
Effectiveness index (survey results 1 to 5)	3.9	4.2	4.5	●
Application downtime (% of total)	1.6	1.5	1.3	●
Intranet services (% of users/theoretical total)	70	85	78	◯

Figure 7.1 Example of a department mission scorecard

by orienting them toward a single end: mission accomplishment.

The personal mission

Several years ago, when we first put forward the idea of MBM, we had an experience that made us think more carefully about each employee's personal mission. A company in the automotive supply industry asked us to train its managers on how to deploy the corporate mission in shared missions. After training, the managers designed an implementation plan and we agreed to meet subsequently to carry out an audit and help them complete the project.

When we went back three months later, we had a surprise. In view of the positive reactions to shared missions, several managers, at their own initiative, had taken the idea further: they had developed personal missions for their subordinates. However, these personal missions had certain undesirable consequences which emerged during the audit phase. Many people saw the company's attempts to define their personal mission as unwarranted interference. The corporate mission, and its deployment in shared missions, was quite different from the personal mission.

Stephen Covey, author of the best-selling *The 7 Habits of Highly Effective People*,[5] describes the personal mission[6] as that which connects a person to "his most genuine purpose and the deep satisfaction derived from fulfilling it."[7] As one would imagine, a personal mission is something more than a corporate mission or a shared mission. Although this book is not about the personal mission, there are three points worth making about how the personal mission is related to and yet different from the shared mission.

1. *The shared mission is not the personal mission*: When we talk about a shared mission, we are talking exclusively about how a person helps to fulfill a corporate mission. In most cases, a person's personal mission will naturally encompass goals other than those of his shared mission.

2. *The shared mission does not override the personal mission*: The fact that a person participates in, or owns, a shared mission does not mean that he cannot also have a personal mission. This is something that managers and employees sometimes forget, as if serving the company were their sole purpose in life. Loss of talent and job conflict are increasingly due to people finding it difficult to combine work and a personal mission.

3. *Shared mission and personal mission must be complementary*: Shared mission is an invitation to each organizational member to make the company's mission part of his personal mission and so share the organization's common purpose. The shared mission thus complements the personal mission, and employees' daily work acquires a genuine sense of contribution and self-realization.

Summing up, employees' personal missions should never be disdained or ignored, as if they had nothing to do with the company. On the contrary, we believe that companies should do their best to help employees fulfill their personal mission. In fact, we believe it is possible to reconcile each employee's personal mission with the corporate mission. Reconciling the two is not just healthy business practice; it will also help a company acquire and retain talent and persuade employees to commit to and identify with the corporate mission and values.

8

Mission management tools

In Chapter 7 we set out our proposal for deploying a mission throughout a company's various functions and levels. However, mission deployment cannot be seen as a simple add-on to existing management systems. If it were, the result would most likely be inconsistent, and the mission would have no real impact on daily activities.

Therefore, the next step, after deploying the mission, is to redesign the company's management systems, so that they are oriented toward the corporate mission. As we saw earlier in this book, in many cases, existing management systems are quite inadequate for putting a company's purpose into effect.

To overcome these shortcomings, we need new management tools that link business interests to people's interests by providing the means to motivate people based on a company's mission and values.

Under this new management system, people will see work not just as "a way to earn a living," but also as a way to contribute to society and realize themselves as individuals.

In recent decades, many management experts have acknowledged the need to redesign "traditional" management tools. The ultimate end of any management system is to fulfill the company's purpose. Every part of the whole must be oriented toward that end. One of the greatest experts in management systems, W. Edwards Deming, reminds us that every system must have a clear and definite purpose: "without a purpose there is no system."[1]

In this chapter, taking the mission as the core of the company, we shall outline our proposal for redesigning some of the principal management tools in use today. These proposals have been tested and implemented in companies of different sizes and in different industries. The results have shown that a strong corporate mission can give traditional management systems focus and consistency.

Without aiming to cover all the management tools a company may or should have, we shall discuss how the four basic tools that drive most management systems can be redesigned:

- Mission and strategy.
- Mission-linked objectives.

- Competency development.

- Performance assessment.

New management tools?

Anyone with a passing interest in management will know that these four tools are not new. They are all thoroughly documented and backed by decades of experience by consultants and practitioners. Ours is an evolutionary proposal: to take these tools a step further by reorienting them to promote a mission and a values-focused approach to business.

In other words, we are not trying to introduce new management tools, but to use the ones we already have as a vehicle for deploying the mission throughout the organization. MBM is intended as a natural development from traditional management tools, not a radical new departure.

By reorienting management systems toward the corporate mission, we also aim to overcome two of the most significant limitations of many management systems today. The first is the tendency to concentrate on tangible measures of success (productivity, profit, asset utilization, etc.), while neglecting intangibles (customer satisfaction, employee motivation, etc.). The second is the excessive focus on individual performance and individual rewards, rather than overall organizational performance.

Mission and strategy: A question of congruence

Mission and strategy are the two most important factors in any company. Through the contribution commitments that define a company's identity, the mission determines "what the company exists for." Corporate strategy sets the goals and lays down the rules for achieving them. Both mission and strategy must be ambitious and, at the same time, a focus of motivation that inspires and encourages people.

In a mission-driven management system, however, mission and strategy are not two separate entities. They must be closely aligned and stand by one another in a *cause–effect relationship*. If mission and strategy are unaligned, organizational members are likely to conflict with one another on a daily basis. Usually, the root of the problem is that the company's mission has not been properly worked out at the strategic level. For example, some pharmaceutical companies have missions such as "to preserve and enhance life" or "to alleviate pain and cure disease"; and yet they describe their strategy as being "to double turnover by 2012." What does "preserving and enhancing life" have to do with "doubling turnover by 2012?" Everything and nothing. A deeply mission-conscious CEO will quickly point out the connection: by doubling turnover and winning more customers, the company accomplishes its mission more effectively and more completely, reaching more people whose life needs preserving and enhancing. But is that what the production manager, the head of sales, or workers on the packaging line understand when they hear the message?

This is not a problem that can be solved by rewording definitions or catchphrases. When mission and strategy are stated correctly, the cause–effect relationship between the two becomes clear: a company accomplishes its mission through its strategy.

The whole company benefits from the organizational congruence that comes from having a mission and strategy that reinforce and complement one another. When a company knows its mission, the various strategies it pursues over time are more likely to be robust and consistent with one another. When the mission is unclear or nonexistent, the company is at the mercy of opportunistic market forces. The mission concentrates the company's efforts and keeps it focused in times of crisis.

At the same time, the mission always demands more from strategy: it demands tangible results. If a strategy does not yield results, the mission will force a change, possibly a radical change. In other words, change does not come about at the whim of some senior executive, eager to prove his worth (and sometimes crippling the company in the process). To the extent that it is genuinely necessary, change is dictated by the mission. On the strength of his experience at Medtronic, CEO William George insisted that "employees can adapt to important strategic changes if the company's mission and values remain intact. In fact, employees are capable of making extraordinary sacrifices provided they trust their leaders implicitly."[2] Strategy changes, the mission abides.

To understand the relationship between mission and strategy, we need to distinguish between three basic theories of strategy formation[3] (Figure 8.1).

The first sees strategy as a result of "deliberate managerial intention." According to this theory, strategy reflects managers' choice among a range of ends and the means to achieve them.

The second theory sees strategy as the outcome of "political and cultural processes." Here, strategy emerges from negotiation and bargaining among internal or external stakeholders, with managers acting as "mediators seeking consensus."

The third view is that strategy is "imposed from outside the organization." This theory holds that managers have very little power to determine strategy, which is shaped mainly by market circumstances and outside agencies.

Figure 8.1 Strategy formation (*Source*: adapted from *Exploring Corporate Strategy*)

Generally speaking, strategic decisions cannot be satisfactorily explained by any one of these theories, but only by a combination of all three. Therefore, to formulate a strategy that is aligned with the company's mission and values, managers must aim for a balance between mission commitments and market and stakeholder pressures.

This means that strategy cannot be defined exclusively from the perspective of competition or external pressure. While strategy must seek to maintain or enhance the company's competitive position (a certain leadership position, for example), it must also ensure that mission commitments are met. Therefore, strategy cannot be considered exclusively from the perspective of external imposition or political processes. To align mission and strategy, it is vital to consider managers' declared willingness to translate the various aspects of the mission into specific strategies.

The strategy time horizon varies widely from company to company. Some companies have detailed strategic plans over a three-, five-, or even ten-year horizon. In today's volatile environment, however, such long-term plans are becoming increasingly questionable. For this reason, some organizations have abandoned long-term planning in favor of guidelines based on a particular *vision* or desire for the future.

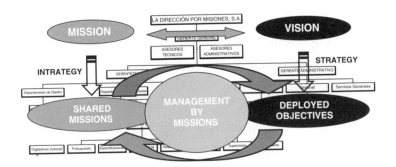

Figure 8.2 Deployment of mission and strategy

At the same time, strategy is presented and communicated to employees differently depending on how centralized a company's culture is, or how empowered middle managers and front-line employees are.

In MBM, as Figure 8.2 shows, the corporate mission is deployed in shared missions, while strategy is deployed in objectives. Mission and strategy should be deployed in parallel, so that they are linked (as in the figure) just as the shared missions are linked to objectives. Then, the congruence between mission and strategy is reproduced throughout the organization, and the objectives are imbued with a stronger "sense of mission." This strategy deployment process, supported by the mission chart, is what we call "mission-linked objectives."

Mission-linked objectives

In the MBM philosophy, mission and objectives are mutually dependent: "a mission without objectives is a dead mission, and an objective without a mission

is a blind objective." As in MBO, objectives are a
key component of the MBM system, but with one
clear proviso: they are meaningful only if they serve
the corporate mission.

It could be argued that objectives are already
implicitly focused on the mission in managers'
minds. However, the focusing needs to be done
explicitly, so as to enrich the entire goal-setting process and give it a mission orientation. A senior bank
executive acknowledged as much: "Although the
bank's mission placed great emphasis on customer
service and staff development, the management
team's objectives were almost exclusively economic
and financial. How can people identify with a richer,
broader mission if their objectives are exclusively
financial? Once it was accepted that objectives
should genuinely serve the mission, it became clear
that the economic and financial objectives needed
to be complemented with mission-oriented objectives, especially in customer service and employee
development."

When the objectives serve the mission, the mission
itself will demand that the objectives be met. Objectives may change significantly, or even completely,
without there being any change in the mission. On
the other hand, some objectives may stay the same
for several periods if the mission is best served that
way. Basically, each person must decide in each
period what objectives he must set himself in order
to most effectively fulfill his mission. Each person

has primary responsibility for goal setting at his own level. Needless to say, the objectives he chooses must be guided – and ultimately approved – by a higher-level manager, as the higher-level manager will not accomplish his own mission unless his subordinates accomplish theirs. Thus, there is a balance between top-down and bottom-up deployment of objectives. A manager may – and sometimes must – impose objectives on his subordinates. But he must also appeal to each person's sense of responsibility and willingness to take the initiative in setting his own goals.

In MBM, the aim is not to achieve more ambitious objectives each year, but to accomplish the mission more completely. Upping objectives by, say, 2 percent or 5 percent will not be enough unless it serves to invest the mission with a real sense of urgency. It may turn out to be necessary to raise the objectives by 50 percent, or lower them by 20 percent. It is the mission that gives meaning to the objectives, not the other way around.

Competency management

Competency management is one of the more recent developments aimed at enriching and complementing traditional management by objectives. While MBO focuses on goal setting ("what to do"), competency management looks at the means to achieve those goals ("how to do it"). Competency systems are designed to help companies evolve toward "a new system combining objectives and competencies"[4] (the "what" and the "how"), competencies being "observable behaviors that contribute to success in a task or function."[5]

In practice, most competency systems have three components:

1. *A competency directory*: This is a fairly concise document in which the company defines the competencies (usually numbering between 10 and 20) that it considers crucial to the success of its business. The directory also describes the observable behaviors resulting from each competency.

2. *A measurement and assessment method*: In line with the notion that "you can't manage what you don't measure," competency systems establish various ways of measuring and assessing organizational members' progress in acquiring certain competencies. Common measurement tools range from simple self-assessment to external assessment involving superiors (90° feedback), subordinates (180° feedback), or peers and customers (360° feedback).

3. *A development plan*: The purpose of the development plan is to reinforce a person's strengths and make good any deficiencies or areas for improvement. Development plans may be implemented at individual, group, or even company level. Three of the most important development tools are training courses, on-the-job training, and coaching.

All such tools are inadequate and ineffective, however, unless people genuinely want to improve. Many competency systems fail precisely because the people who are supposed to acquire certain competencies do not see why they should. Therefore, the first step in any competency management system is to get people to accept the need for them to acquire certain competencies in order for the mission to be accomplished.

In 1988, Boeing published and distributed among its employees a document that listed, in the form of clear and specific behaviors, the competencies that every Boeing manager was expected to develop. This list, based on a system known as "Corporate Direction," similar to the mission and values, bore the title "Desirable Characteristics of Managers." Five years later, Boeing Chairman Frank Shrontz received a letter from employees saying that while the list of behaviors seemed reasonable, it bore little relation to the way people actually behaved in the company. As a corrective measure, Shrontz first scrubbed the word "desirable" from the document title. He then established a management tool whereby each manager would send a questionnaire to his superiors, peers, and subordinates asking them to assess his performance in relation to the competencies and behaviors listed in "Characteristics of Managers." This made Boeing a pioneer in the use of competency systems.

The MBM system, based on many such examples, is described in Cardona and García-Lombardía's recent book *How to Develop Leadership Competencies.*

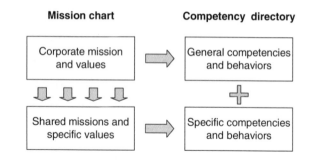

Figure 8.3   Competency directory

A competency system must reflect the company's cultural values and mission. Otherwise it risks being seen as an arbitrary imposition (the whim of a consultant or parent company management), meaning nothing to the company's members.

In MBM, a company's competency system is derived from the company's mission and shared missions (Figure 8.3). Based on the corporate mission and values, we define a set of general competencies that apply to the whole company. Then, based on the shared missions and specific values, we define specific competencies, which are adapted to the particularities of each area or department.

The MBM system also gives managers a new responsibility in the form of what we earlier termed the "managerial mission": to contribute to the development of subordinates. This means that coaching is one of the basic functions of any manager. A manager must see to it that "his subordinates realize their potential and develop their professional capabilities."[6]

Performance assessment

There is a direct relationship between the way a company is managed and the way employee performance is evaluated. Specifically, we can distinguish three different assessment methods, depending on a company's management system and leadership styles.

In *management by tasks* we find the "command-and-control" type of manager, who manages people through strict task and role assignments. This type of manager is unlikely to carry out a good performance assessment; instead, he will merely correct mistakes when subordinates fail to carry out their tasks exactly as required. This way of managing people tends to foster a reactive attitude in subordinates, who are afraid of making mistakes and so do the bare minimum. As a result, employees' potential and motivation is wasted.

A more advanced system is MBO, in which managers are encouraged to delegate and subordinates are encouraged to assume responsibilities. In MBO, each employee works in a context defined by certain objectives, which are his responsibility; he accepts them as a challenge and pursue them proactively. Performance assessment is not confined to correcting mistakes. Performance measurement is centered on the degree of achievement of mutually agreed objectives. Although MBO has proven effective, it still has serious limitations when it comes to developing employees' full potential. Because employees' efforts and energy are focused entirely on achieving agreed objectives, they tend to lose sight of the big picture or the needs of the whole.

Management by missions overcomes these limitations through what we call "integral assessment," which is centered on employees' contribution and development. MBM combines goal achievement with other qualitative or intangible factors, such as personal behavior and competency development. In MBM, we assess the way each employee contributes to the accomplishment of the company's mission. To do that, we use a system of assessment, mission centred in which intangible factors may carry as much weight as tangible or quantitative measures. In the case of a sales manager, for example, assessment, mission centred does not merely count the contribution to sales; it also measures other outcomes that are equally important to the accomplishment of the manager's mission, such as collaboration with other departments, internal and external customer satisfaction, or the development of particular leadership skills.

Assessment, mission centred under MBM is an effective way to develop each person's potential to the full, while serving the company's mission. The focus on results remains, but there is also a broader view, taking in the longer term and the organization's values. Any company that succeeds in implementing assessment, mission centred inevitably acquires a competitive advantage.

Management system	What is assessed?	Expected performance
Management by tasks	Mistakes	Minimal for fear of making mistakes
Management by objectives	Actual results	Fulfillment of agreed objectives
Management by missions	Mission contribution and competency development.	Full realization of potential

We should warn, however, that for assessment, mission centred to work, the company must abandon any attempt to link the assessment only with financial incentives. Although such a linkage is possible in MBO, as the assessment is based on objective, measurable results, it would not be appropriate to tie variable pay to subjective factors.

For this reason, in MBM we recommend that financial incentives be linked exclusively to performance that can be measured or quantified. In the case of an employee's mission contribution, incentives will have to be linked to quantifiable results. In the case of personal competency development, incentives will have to be linked to the personal development plan, setting specific parameters for measuring plan completion and effectiveness.

In fact, some authors recommend that qualitative factors be assessed separately from quantitative factors and at a different time of year, so as to avoid any association between the two. Whatever practice a company adopts, assessment must not be seen as a form of wage negotiation, but as an exercise designed to help accomplish the mission and develop competencies.

Redesign of other management tools

Besides the tools already mentioned, there are others that we have tried to redesign in recent years to make them more mission-oriented. Examples include the selection process, orientation manuals, training plans, internal and external communication policies, career plans, ethics codes, flexibility and social responsibility policies, and so on.

The purpose of redefining these tools, as with the four tools we have discussed in depth, is to make the mission the center of the entire management system. Thus, as the redesigned tools come into use in day-to-day management, the mission becomes more tangible and the company more congruent at all levels.

Management systems and leadership

When we started to implement MBM in organizations in various industries, we soon realized that it is more than just a set of management tools. MBM generates real cultural change which affects the way top and middle managers manage people.

This is something we had anticipated in theory when we began to develop MBM. In practice, however, the changes happened much faster and went much deeper than we expected. Seeing how MBM transforms leaders and their organizations, we have come to the conclusion that cultural change follows a common pattern. This common pattern can be reduced to two basic levers: MBM tools as drivers of change; and the leader as a change facilitator.

MBM tools as drivers of change

With the right leadership, a fundamental change in management systems can bring about a change of culture (Figure 8.4). An example of such a transformation is the change many companies underwent when they introduced MBO. MBO entails a transition from a "command-and-control" culture to one of empowerment, in which employee responsibility is encouraged through delegation.

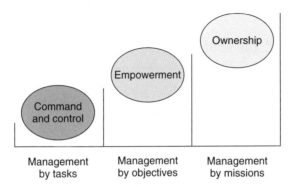

Figure 8.4 Management system and cultures

We have witnessed a similar transforming power at work in the MBM implementations we have been involved in. When mission and values are deployed throughout an organization, people quickly understand that their situation has changed and start to see their work and what is expected of them in a different light.

Just as MBO promotes a culture of empowerment, MBM fosters a new type of leadership capable of creating what might be termed an "ownership culture," in that it encourages employees to accept the company's mission and values as their own.

This is not to say that employees are any less empowered under MBM than they are under MBO. Just as MBO builds on the command-and-control culture, MBM enriches empowerment, giving it more substance and, most importantly, more motivating power.

The leader as a change facilitator

In MBM, the leader is a facilitator of change, providing a *common thread* of ownership throughout the company. He does this by encouraging his team to become leaders in their own right, so that they adopt the company's mission as their own and pass it on to their subordinates. Without this common thread, all the potential for change that an MBM system unleashes merely burns up effort and energy and has no real impact on people. Consequently, managers with mission responsibility must act as mission-driven leaders.

It is not enough for systems and leadership to be connected in just some managers, or just some areas or levels. For MBM to generate tangible results, a company's management systems must be connected, first, with the top level of the organization and then, in cascade, with every other level. Every manager must be a mission bearer and a model to his subordinates. His task is not complete until his subordinates have become leaders.

That is why MBM is implemented "top-down," starting from the CEO and top management. Cultural change is a learning process based on internal consistency between systems and leadership. Therefore, every leader is a change facilitator, and systems and leadership form a coherent whole that can transform the culture of an entire organization.

For management by missions to reach people and a real cultural change to take place, leadership and management systems must be mission-driven and consistent with one another, creating a virtuous circle in which both are reinforced (Figure 8.5). Thus, the management system fosters leadership, and leaders exploit the management system to best effect.

This virtuous circle reflects the essence of management by missions: management systems that

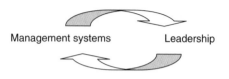

Management systems   Leadership

Figure 8.5 Virtuous circle

turn the mission and the values into a living reality for all the organization's members; and mission-driven leadership that fosters employee commitment and identification with the mission.

9

Mission-driven leadership

The meaning of the term "leadership" has changed significantly since the early twentieth century. The leadership literature has gradually abandoned the personality-centric conception of the leader to include the person or people who are led. In recent years, leadership has been defined as a "relationship of influence" in which both leaders and followers play an important role.[1] This approach focuses on the relationship a leader builds with his followers. Various modern leadership models belong within this relational approach. The best known of them is transformational leadership. However, the limitations of this model are becoming increasingly apparent.

In this chapter we describe the type of leadership that is needed in order to manage by missions: transcendental leadership. Transcendental leadership belongs among the relational models and is intended to enrich transformational leadership. Here, we shall consider in more detail a form of transcendental leadership that we have developed specifically for management by missions. We call it "mission-driven leadership" (MDL).

Leadership types

We can distinguish three types of leadership according to the nature of the influence a leader exerts on his followers:[2] transactional, transformational, and transcendental.

Transactional leadership

Transactional leadership is built on a relationship of economic influence. A transactional leader relies on rewards and punishments to motivate his subordinates. In fact, his ability to influence people depends on his ability to give or withhold incentives. To do that, he lays down clear rules and sets carefully designed objectives. His management style tends to be "command-and-control," with the accent on control and robust use of formal power. He pays close attention to the short term and uses processes and resources efficiently.

A transactional leader is therefore a good manager who seeks continuous improvement through standardization, organization, and repetition of tried and tested processes. Good transactional leaders tend to be good negotiators: they are authoritarian, even aggressive, in getting maximum benefit out of the relationship of economic influence they have created. And yet that benefit is suboptimal from the point of view of other, higher-value-added relationships, because even in the best of cases it includes only the employee behaviors that are part of the formal job requirements.

Transformational leadership

Transformational leadership is based on a relationship of professional influence. In a professional relationship, the subordinate is interested not only in salary and benefits, but also in the job as such: the challenge it offers, what he expects to learn from it, and its overall appeal. The influence exerted by a transformational leader goes deeper than that of a transactional leader, as a transformational leader is able to influence people not only through rewards and punishments, but also by offering an attractive job in which subordinates will learn and commit to tasks. A transformational leader is usually nonconformist, visionary, and charismatic. He repeatedly questions the way things are done in the company and his followers' aspirations and ideals. He is an excellent communicator. Compelling and persuasive, he has great faith in himself and his vision, and pursues the changes he has decided upon with great determination and energy.

The transformational leader is not necessarily opposed to the transactional leader: he is an enriched transactional leader. "Transformational leadership is an extension of transactional leadership."[3] This is the type of leadership advocated by authors such as W.G. Bennis:[4] "[Leaders] know what they want, why they want it and how to communicate what they want to others, so as to win their cooperation and support." Transformational leaders get people to identify with them and their vision, and then empower them to pursue their objectives independently. There is a clear distinction between the leader and his followers: there is only one leader, everyone else is a follower. We could say that the transformational leader *retains* leadership at the top of the pyramid: the leader is the guarantor of the corporate vision and the driver of organizational change. This makes it difficult to develop new leaders within the organization.

Transformational leadership can be especially problematic when the leader's personal vision becomes an end in itself or, worse still, an exercise in self-aggrandizement. The literature is full of examples of leaders who carried people with them for their own personal glory. This is what is often referred to as *narcissistic leadership*.[5] The danger of the narcissistic leader is that he can be manipulative in his efforts to persuade people to do what he wants. To deal with this dark side of the transformational leader, Bass draws a distinction between authentic transformational leadership and pseudo-transformational leadership.[6] Authentic transformational leaders have ethical principles as well as charisma, whereas pseudo-transformational leaders succumb to narcissistic temptation. However, this is a somewhat flimsy distinction. Basically, it shows that another category is needed in order to distinguish authentic from pseudo-transformational leadership.

Transcendental leadership

Transcendental leadership is built on a relationship of personal influence. In a personal relationship, employees are motivated not only by the financial reward and inherent interest of their job; they also have a personal commitment to the leader to accomplish a worthwhile common mission. The influence exerted by a transcendental leader is even deeper than that of a transformational leader, because a transcendental leader is able to influence people not only by giving out rewards and punishments or interesting professional challenges, but also by appealing to their awareness of how other people need them to do their job well, out of a sense of mission. The transcendental leader is strongly committed to a *content-rich* project and makes his subordinates realize how their work contributes to the completion of that project. He preaches by example, which enhances his *credibility* among his subordinates. Lastly, he radiates a powerful sense of *urgency* and encourages his subordinates to accept leadership responsibilities, so that they set themselves demanding and ambitious goals in the service of the corporate mission.

The transcendental leader does not retain leadership at the top; he does his best to ensure that leadership permeates the entire organization. *He is a leader who makes leaders.* He does this by inspiring a sense of mission in his subordinates, each at his particular level of responsibility. The resulting sense of ownership goes deeper than the empowerment championed by transformational leaders. A transcendental leader sees his work as a service to his subordinates, so that they, in turn, may accomplish the mission at their level. Essentially, the transcendental leader is at the service of the mission. For that reason, he is more detached from his own opinions, even from his own job, should the mission so require. As a leader of leaders, he expects his subordinates to take on more responsibility and prefers to share any successes with them, rather than taking all the credit himself. The transcendental leader could be said to be both more ambitious and more humble than the transformational leader.[7]

Mission-driven leadership

In practice, there have been certain managers who could be considered *examples* of what we have defined as transcendental leadership: leaders who make leaders. Many of them are widely studied and admired and are held up as models. We have already mentioned David Packard of HP, R.W. Johnson of Johnson & Johnson, and Tom Watson of IBM. Mostly, they are people with exceptional, out-of-the-ordinary qualities who surround themselves with a team of leaders. They have deeply rooted personal principles and values that enable them to achieve what so many companies wish for nowadays: employees who are committed to a content-rich, credible, and urgent mission.

And yet, these are precisely exceptional cases, exceptional people, exceptional achievements. Very likely the reader will have wondered, What about the rest of us – managers, supervisors, team leaders – who have not been blessed with exceptional gifts? Is it unrealistic to promote transcendental leadership in ordinary organizations? Is transcendental leadership reserved for a select few "textbook" cases? Our experience in developing and implementing management by missions suggests that it is not.

In our consulting work with organizations of different sizes and in different industries, we have found that transcendental leadership is possible and attainable at all levels, provided the context is right. This is where MBM comes into the picture, as MBM generates a particular form of transcendental leadership which we have called MDL. In MDL, to *manage people* is to turn them into leaders who will take ownership of the mission at their level and accomplish it excellently. Unlike transformational leadership, MDL can be extended to all levels of the organization.

In MBM, it is not a matter of leading departments, or divisions, or even people. In MBM, every manager, at every level, leads a *mission*; that is what makes him a leader. It is not that the mission-driven leader has exceptional qualities or a special charisma. MDL is directly related to a mission and values that transcend the person of the leader. That is why in this chapter we shall use the term "leader" to refer to any person – CEO, manager, or middle manager – who has mission responsibility. A leader is any person who has direct responsibility for carrying out a mission in which his subordinates participate.

Dimensions of MDL

In MBM, as we have explained, management tools are the driver, while the leader is the facilitator, of cultural change in the company. In other words, cultural change does not come about automatically just because a company uses certain tools. It is a learning process in which managers and subordinates gradually acquire new knowledge, attitudes, and behaviors, until everybody accepts responsibility for leading the mission at his particular level. In implementing MBM in a variety of companies, we have developed and tested a model of how a manager can become a mission-driven leader. This model is structured in three basic dimensions: commitment, cooperation, and change.

Commitment

Mission-driven leadership starts with measures to foster employee commitment. One of the main effects MBM has on an organization is the enrichment of the employer–employee relationship. To the basic employment relationship – be it extrinsic (work for money) or intrinsic (satisfaction of the challenge) – MBM adds the transcendent relationship of commitment (employees feel they have a part in the mission that is to be accomplished). As the leader follows the steps shown in Figure 9.1, subordinates start to accept a mission commitment, in addition to their interest in the job itself or the pay and benefits.

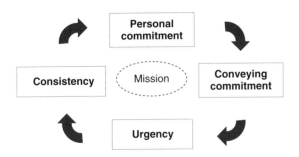

Figure 9.1 Cycle of commitment

1. *Personal commitment.* The first factor facilitating an ownership culture is the leader's personal commitment, whatever his position in the hierarchy. Unlike empowerment, which varies with a person's rank, mission commitment can be essentially the same in a general manager, a middle manager, or a shop-floor worker.

   When the mission is deployed in shared missions, top and middle managers must reflect on their personal commitment to the company's mission and values. The mission cannot be said to have been deployed successfully until the leader fully accepts and assumes this commitment through a shared mission. It is not enough, therefore, for top and middle managers to accept their shared missions as a "theoretical" necessity. They need to commit to their assigned missions by getting personally involved. Then, the shared mission becomes a matter of personal commitment. The leaders' personal commitment, starting right at the top of the organization, is a prerequisite for the next stage in the process: conveying commitment to subordinates.

2. *Conveying commitment*. One of the main conclusions we have drawn from our experience with MBM is that people usually find the idea of participating in a common mission and values highly attractive. This means that leaders often find that their subordinates are open to what they have to say and keen to participate in the company's mission and values. For this provisional interest to harden into genuine commitment, however, the leaders must demonstrate a strong commitment of their own. Even if subordinates are initially skeptical, they will eventually accept the mission and commit to it if their leader shows real conviction. To inspire commitment in his subordinates, a leader must convey their own personal commitment in such a way that his subordinates can see it and "feel" it. For that to happen, he must organize his communication with his subordinates around the mission and values, seizing every opportunity to relate what they do to "what they are doing it for." By contrast, if communication revolves around achieving certain objectives, subordinates will interpret those objectives as an end in themselves, rather than as a means to circumscribe and advance toward the end, which is the mission. A manager who concentrates on objectives, rather than on conveying commitment, denies people's work its full meaning and connection with the company's mission. A manager can only convey mission commitment if he shows a real concern that goes beyond achieving objectives. Given time, commitment becomes an unwritten rule in the

company and a precondition for integration and belonging. The next step in this process is to distill this commitment into a sense of urgency.

3. *Creating a sense of urgency.* In order to convert commitment into outstanding performance, the leader must create a sense of urgency that directs his subordinates' commitment toward specific, demanding challenges. In MBM, a leader has various tools for generating a sense of urgency, including mission-linked objectives, missionlinked competencies, and mission centered assessment.

   To create a real sense of urgency, however, the leader must always demand *mission-driven excellence*. This is very different from excellence driven by utilitarian considerations (to maximize profits) or the exercise of power ("because I say so"). To demand mission-driven excellence is to create an urgency to accomplish a certain mission and certain values to which leader and subordinates alike have committed. When a leader demands mission-driven excellence and creates a real sense of urgency, the management tools leadership combination is reinforced and generates outstanding performance in the service of the mission. But this means staying on course, without being deflected or discouraged by whatever difficulties may emerge over time, which brings us to the fourth element of our model: consistency.

4. *Acting consistently.* When referring to the mission and values, consistency means two complementary things. First, it means consistency among the

various components of a mission. For example, if a mission includes the basic commitments to customers, shareholders, and employees, the leader must treat all three stakeholder groups with an equally high sense of commitment, without neglecting any one in favor of another (although priorities will naturally differ at any given moment). The same applies to values: concentrating on one value and neglecting others would generate what we referred to earlier as dysfunctional cultures.

Secondly, consistency has to do with a leader's perseverance over time. The three behaviors we have described – personal commitment, conveying commitment, and creating a sense of urgency – are not occasional or temporary efforts. A leader must practice them resolutely and constantly. If the leader does not persevere, his subordinates are very unlikely to follow his example, and all the initial effort to secure commitment and create a sense of urgency will be wasted. Perseverance is not just about maintaining commitment; it also means continually renewing and reinforcing commitment at the personal level, which brings us back to the start of the cycle.

Cooperation

Cooperation – between areas, departments, and individual employees – is in huge demand in companies today. People in business are forever talking about team work, collaboration, and internal customers; or comparing the company to an orchestra or sports team. These are all ways of highlighting the fact that for a company to succeed, there has to be a *certain amount* of cooperation. Yet, after decades of trying to instill cooperation through training courses, incentives, assessment systems, employee-of-the-month awards, and so on, the results are, on the whole, unsatisfactory.

In our opinion, the root of the problem is fairly obvious, or at least easy to identify. Lack of cooperation between people is a direct consequence of the lack of *motives to cooperate*.[8] Usually, it is not because people lack the necessary resources, or time, or knowledge; they are simply "not interested" in cooperating. To cooperate, people need to have a reason or motive to cooperate. But motives to cooperate are only sustainable when they are transcendent motives.[9] That is because cooperating always means going beyond one's own interests, transcending one's self.

Management by mission goes to the root of the problem of cooperation. With the help of shared missions and interdependencies, MBM generates a solid foundation of motives to cooperate that fosters the attitudes required for effective cooperation. However, for the system to actually generate cooperative attitudes, managers must complete the leadership process illustrated in Figure 9.2.

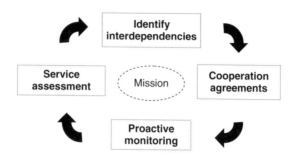

Figure 9.2   Cycle of cooperation

1. *Identify interdependencies*. In MBM, the leader must know who his internal customers are, and what their needs are, within the framework of the company's mission. This is very different from satisfying personal needs or doing things to please everybody. Identifying needs within the mission framework consists of determining what a person or department must do in order to contribute more effectively to the company's mission.

Therefore, when a mission-driven leader identifies a need, he must understand how that need ties in with the corporate mission. So when we explain our need to another, interdependent area, we can say, "It's not me who's asking," it is the corporate mission that requires this particular act of cooperation. Within the mission framework, we can distinguish the following three types of cooperation needs.

Horizontal cooperation needs: Needs for cooperation between two or more areas of the company. Horizontal cooperation is based on what we earlier called the "mission value chain" and is structured according to interdependencies. This chain describes how the different areas cooperate to accomplish the company's mission.

Vertical cooperation needs: Needs for cooperation between managers and subordinates. Vertical cooperation consists of mutual support between managers and subordinates when addressing the resources, information sharing, training, coaching, and so on needed to accomplish the subordinates' shared mission.

Group cooperation needs: Needs for cooperation between members of the same department. The leader is responsible for promoting cooperation among the members of his team. This means, among other things, promoting team spirit, not creating internal rivalry, encouraging communication, resolving conflicts, and so on.

2. *Create cooperation agreements.* Once he has identified the cooperation needs, the leader must find a way to satisfy them effectively. For that, customer and supplier must reach an agreement by negotiating expectations.[10] It is important to approach the negotiation with an open mind and a willingness to listen to the parties and set priorities from a mission-linked process perspective.

What is different in MBM is that this negotiation process must be centered on the company's mission and values (which is where the motives to cooperate come from). For a mission-driven leader, negotiating expectations must lead to true commitments to support the other person's shared mission. These agreements must be clarified and spelled out, preferably in formal documents.[11] In some cases, the commitment may be specified through indicators such as minimum inventory levels required in order for Sales to deliver a given service level. In other cases, however, such as information sharing between departments, it may be better to leave the commitment more open. In any case, the spirit of these agreements is not one of control or blame, but of a desire for effectiveness and efficiency in internal service between areas. Accordingly, for such agreements to be genuinely useful, there has to be the third element of our model: proactive monitoring.

3. *Monitor proactively.* To create a real culture of cooperation, it is not enough merely to formally specify inter-area commitments. The leader must foster among his team, and in his environment, a true culture of mutual learning through proactive monitoring. Proactive monitoring should help us to identify new opportunities for cooperation in our various relationships. Over time, the needs of interdependencies may vary and change, either naturally or as a result of internal reorganization or changes in the environment. This means that merely satisfying certain cooperation agreements is not enough; expectations and commitments must be adjusted to fit current circumstances, and any misadjustments must be corrected.

For that to happen, there have to be channels of communication and an attitude of trust to allow feedback among parties. On various occasions we have come across organizations with "opaque" and inefficient management, which makes any such feedback difficult. Removing this opacity is one of MBM's main tasks. In MBM, departmental meetings are usually also attended by interdependent areas. This way, each area receives periodic feedback on its internal service level and suggestions as to how it could make its service more effective. Thus, sharing the area mission at regular intervals and explaining the area's needs to other areas becomes second nature and part of the company's culture.

4. *Assess the service.* In MBM, every employee is assessed on his direct or indirect contribution to the accomplishment of the corporate mission. This means that leaders and their subordinates are assessed, among other things, on their contribution to other areas apart from their own. Also, the assessment is carried out by the people best qualified in each case. For example, internal service is assessed by internal customers.

The purpose of assessment is to diagnose faults constructively, with a view to ongoing improvement, not to pass judgment and apportion blame. Judgment looks to the past, whereas diagnosis looks to the future. The important thing is to learn to cooperate better and more efficiently out of a sense of mission. Then, it will be possible to detect new needs that had not been considered, or that had not been given the necessary priority. And so we come back to the start of the cycle.

Change

The competencies and talent needed to accomplish a company's mission with excellence are constantly evolving, as the needs and expectations of customers, employees, shareholders, and other stakeholders evolve. A car buyer today has very different expectations from the one 20 years ago, and expectations will be very different again 20 years from now. The same applies to the needs and expectations of a company's employees. A mission may remain "untouched" for decades; but the way to accomplish that mission excellently will be constantly changing. On the other hand, we must also beware of falling into the opposite trap: change for change's sake. MDL fosters change at all levels, provided the mission requires it. The process starts with personal change and follows the steps described in Figure 9.3.

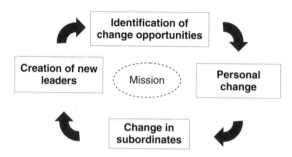

Figure 9.3 Cycle of change

1. *Identification of change opportunities.* When a leader is personally committed to a mission – with a sense of urgency and consistency – a real ambition, beyond short-term interests, takes control: a quest for excellence. Excellence is an organization's highest virtue, by which the organization's members strive at all times to perform their mission more fully and more effectively. Mission commitment demands excellence, and excellence leads to change, in a constant effort to improve and develop the organization.

   In the pursuit of excellence, change is not an end, but a means (this is perhaps the most important thing to remember when attempting any change). The quest is never-ending and requires a constant balance between exploitation and exploration.[12] Excellence shuns frivolous change as much as it does unnecessary rigidity. Both are an obstacle to progress toward mission completion. To achieve excellence, therefore, change must be driven by a deep sense of mission, in a constant striving to more effectively fulfill the company's commitments to customers, employees, shareholders, and other key stakeholders.

   While it is true that the mission provides a basic stability for the organization's identity and development, such stability is not to be confused with stagnation, much less rigidity. The mission requires constant review of the way things are done, offering scope for ambitious and daring approaches that could scarcely be justified based on short-term objectives. It stimulates people to continue with their efforts once they have started, even though the efforts may not yield immediate benefits and may sometimes depart from prevailing trends. In fact, even in strategies of continuity, excellence always seeks new approaches and attitudes to accomplish the mission ever more effectively.

A leader who is committed to a mission – be it the corporate mission or a shared mission – takes the lead and drives change, seeking constant evolution to meet the demands of mission excellence. This combination of mission and excellence is the key to the transformation which starts with personal change.

2. *Personal change.* The pursuit of mission excellence drives change – new ideas, new products, new services, new organizations – in a word, new ways of doing things. But ultimately, what changes is not companies, structures, or processes, but people – and, first and foremost, the leader who drives the change. Once the new path has been chosen, the leader is the first to walk it.

Leadership requires a continuous personal balance between building on what is already there and investing in new approaches and competencies. Experience is important, provided it does not hinder progress toward a better paradigm. In any case, the mission requires a constant attitude of learning. In this learning path, the leader must have the courage to explore new paths, overcoming any uncertainty this may entail. Besides courage, he must also practice the humility that any learning process requires: know how to listen; accept help; try new methods; try again, without being discouraged, if he fails first time; and so on.

A mission-driven leader does not cling to his assumptions (given that the mission, not he, will guide the change); nor is he afraid of losing his authority if he admits his mistakes. On the contrary, he bases his prestige on a constant effort to improve himself in whatever way is necessary in order to accomplish the mission. This learning process is greatly assisted if the leader always has a personal improvement plan containing specific measures targeting the areas in which he must improve in order to more effectively fulfill his mission. This personal improvement plan shows the development objectives that drive change at the personal level. We have even come across leaders who openly share their personal improvement plan with their subordinates, encouraging them to provide feedback and assistance.

3. *Promote change in subordinates.* Once the personal change is under way, even though it is a long process that has barely begun, the leader has the necessary authority to try to change his subordinates. Mission excellence is not something a person can achieve on his own, but only together with other people. Therefore, the change has to be propagated from the top down, in a coordinated way.

Many managers try to get their subordinates to change, but the changes tend to be superficial: people adapt to the new requirements out of obedience, or even trust in their boss, but without taking on board the deeper reasons for the change. Often this is because their boss focuses on results and does not emphasize the mission and the mission requirements. Nor does the boss take enough interest in his subordinates' needs or the difficulties they have in coping with change.

The crucial thing, at this stage, is for subordinates to progress from merely *adapting* to change to actually *internalizing* it. This is achieved when they see the change as necessary for mission excellence. It is the mission that demands change, and it is employees' mission commitment that must drive the efforts and learning required to make the mission happen. Just as the leader must have a personal improvement plan, so too must his subordinates. Just as employees pursue their personal improvement plan with a sense of mission, they also internalize change.

This change process is an exercise in *coaching*. The leader must be a coach to his team: somebody close with whom team members can discuss the problems and needs they face in promoting mission-driven change. Only then can leaders help their people to really internalize the changes that are needed in order to accomplish the mission with excellence. For this reason, the leader must always find time in his agenda to coach his subordinates.

4. *Create new leaders.* The change is complete when the leader's followers become promoters of change, that is, leaders in their own right. Of all the steps in the change process, this is the one that takes longest. The subordinate becomes a leader, and the leader becomes a leader of leaders. The mission-driven leader does not lead "from the top"; he passes the baton of leadership to his subordinates and on down, in cascade, to the base of the organization.

Exactly how MBM generates new leaders, level by level, is unclear. What we have observed, however, is that leadership spreads down the organization as subordinates progress from simply internalizing change to actually promoting it. Deploying the mission in shared missions is a key factor in this process. As we said previously, it is the mission that turns a boss into a leader. And as bosses intensify their personal commitment to the shared mission at their level, the pursuit of excellence, personal change, and change promotion cascade through the organization. Every leader seeks excellence in mission fulfillment at his level and promotes the necessary change.

Then, as the mission is deployed in shared missions, the concern to detect possible improvements and to innovate so as to accomplish the mission with excellence becomes more than just an issue for top management. Each leader, at his level, seeks excellence in the performance of his mission, promoting the necessary changes to achieve it. Thus, through change promotion, subordinates start to see the mission with the eyes of leaders and discover new challenges and bold ideas for accomplishing the mission even more effectively. And so a new cycle of change begins, in a continual pursuit of excellence.

The leadership model we have presented, which we call MDL, is not a theoretical model written up in an office. On the contrary, it is a structured representation of processes that we have observed and consolidated by implementing MBM in a range of companies. As we pointed out earlier, MBM requires a particular type of leadership – transcendental leadership – to really bring about cultural change. At the same time, however, MBM facilitates the emergence of transcendental leaders. In other words, MDL is the natural result of effective implementation of MBM.

This is not to say that MDL will necessarily be achieved in its fullest form. Leadership is always a form of self-realization, the result of many victories, and defeats accepted sportingly and with a readiness to learn. That is why any MBM implementation requires the support of a serious and sustained program of leadership training and coaching. Ultimately, one can never claim that MDL has been achieved for once and for all. People and circumstances change and the process will need to be reinforced again and again. But we can safely say that, properly implemented, MBM brings about a significant change in the organization and its leadership. In the next chapter we shall describe in some detail how MBM can be implemented in a company. We will see how MBM and leadership interact to bring about cultural change.

10

CASE: Sony Spain, the implementation

Today, many companies already have practical experience of MBM. On the one hand, more than 50 companies have been through our training courses and are applying our ideas to some extent in their organizations. Then there are the managers who have read our publications and have adapted our ideas to their organizations. Some of them, have contacted us and we regularly exchange experiences and analyze their progress. Lastly, there are the companies on which we have conducted consultancy projects on strategy and cultural change based on MBM, some of which have resulted in a complete cultural transformation.

From this latter group, we have chosen Sony España as a practical example for this book. It is a particularly significant case because Sony España was one of the first companies we helped to design, manage, and execute a cultural change project based on MBM. This also means there has been plenty of time to assess the results and situate them in a medium-term perspective.

At the company's request, we have deliberately omitted the details of Sony's strategy and concentrate exclusively on the implementation of MBM.

The starting situation at Sony España

Market situation

Having led the field in practically all its products and markets for decades, Sony España was facing a much more challenging environment. Competition from private label and Chinese imports was intensifying and the level of professionalism among retailers and competitors was increasing.

There had been signs in recent years that the company was starting to lose its leading position. It was not a sudden drop, but rather a sequence of small warning signs, suggesting that clouds were gathering.

Internal situation

At the same time, the company was weakened from within, with some managers and supervisors comfortably accommodated in their jobs. As sales director Francisco Juan (aged 61, 25 years at Sony) explained, "Before, circumstances had always worked in our favor. When circumstances changed, we started to lose market share because we weren't up with the new technologies in some products. So the whole corporate machine started to creak. Changes were suggested and we launched the MBM project. Before, we had MBO. But some divisions had turned into little fiefdoms, where everyone did strictly and exclusively what they were required to do, without looking to see what people were doing in the division next door. Now, one of our objectives is to break silos and work horizontally. We had a very bureaucratic way of doing things, which sometimes made you feel you were working in a different company."

Another Sony executive, communications director Juan José del Castillo (aged 38, 13 years' service), recalled, "Before the MBM project, people felt demotivated. They didn't want to get involved. In some departments there was an attitude like 'Things are the way they are and it's not going to change, because it's always been like this . . . '. Obviously, that was holding us back. People were demoralized and didn't want to get involved. We were doing 60 percent of top speed, when we could have been doing 100 percent or 120 percent. After all, why work harder if it's not appreciated and doesn't make any difference? Particularly if the project you're working on is quite likely to be axed at any moment or is being mismanaged. This change the company has undertaken was badly needed."

In fact, as Juan José confessed, "I think the workforce is crucial in every company; they keep the company going. We may have excellent products; but what good is it having excellent products if our sales force isn't sufficiently motivated and doesn't push our products hard enough or show the necessary enthusiasm? So people matter, right down to the person who answers the phone and offers his advice, or the person who feels encouraged because he sees that the company is listening, and he knows he has good ideas and there's a chance his ideas will be implemented. That person will look for solutions. He'll be a source of new ideas."

General management

Faced with this situation, Pedro Navarrete, CEO of Sony España (aged 49, 16 years at Sony), decided to adopt a new strategy. He realized that, first, there had to be a change in the organizational culture. Pedro had anticipated the clouds on the horizon and had taken steps to reinforce the culture by launching a change program based on the corporate mission. This mission was built around "the 3 Ps," which were the three pillars of Sony España's value contribution: product, productivity, and people (Exhibit 10.1). In other words, efforts had been made to bring about cultural change using traditional methods based on communication, symbols, leadership and empowerment, and so on, with the idea of moving beyond MBO. However, Pedro realized that the change was not happening fast enough to allow the new strategy to be implemented.

Initially, Pedro Navarrete was convinced that the company needed a change of direction. As he saw

Exhibit 10.1 SONY España's mission

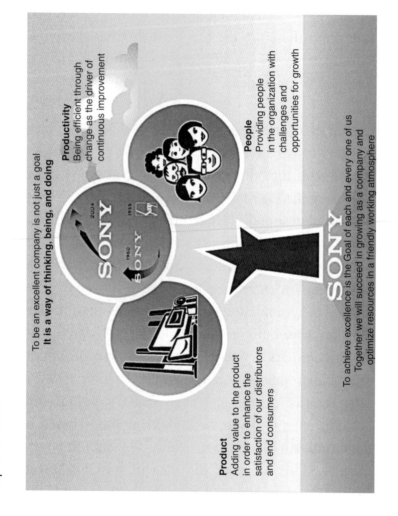

it, the question was, "Why should Sony España exist as a sales subsidiary?" If we're simply a company that distributes certain products, the parent company might just as well deal with a wholesaler. So he asked himself why Sony España and the whole organization in Spain should exist. And his conclusion was that it existed in order to add value! So, in order to add value in the prevailing economic climate, with the way the market was changing, tougher competition and so on, Sony España needed to add value to the product it received. After all, we're a very simple company: we receive merchandise and we deliver it to customers. So Pedro had the idea that excellence, achieved through core objectives, would enable the company to add the necessary value. Sony España had to continue to grow faster than the market, maintain a reasonable expense ratio by European standards, and have employees who were committed to making the business work. So Pedro asked himself, "How are we going to achieve all this?" The answer was, "Through the 3 P's: product, productivity, people."

Discovery of MBM

Sergi García (aged 33, 7 years at Sony) recalled a meeting with Pedro Navarrete in which this issue had been discussed. "When Pedro talked to me about the mission and the 3 P's as a way of adding value, I said to him, 'I totally agree that we've neglected the people dimension.' That's why we had employees who were highly motivated extrinsically and intrinsically, but the 'transcendent motivation' (which was a term I'd never heard of until then) just wasn't there. Around that time, by one of those coincidences, I stumbled across a short-focused program on management by missions at IESE."

After the course, Sergi had another talk with Pedro Navarrete. This time he had some new arguments at his disposal. "You see, in a value creation system, everything depends on people's being willing to add value. And for people to be willing to add value, they need to have more transcendent motivation. However much market strategy and however many new business ideas we have, we're not going to achieve anything unless people are sufficiently motivated. That's where MBM came into the picture and we started to give it serious thought."

Pedro Navarrete thought it was a good idea and Sony management agreed to launch a coordinated campaign on several fronts, so that all this talk of cultural change would lead to actual changes on the ground. Pedro and Sergi started to draw up an action plan for the next two years. The basic framework was built around MBM and based on employee development and communication. To start with, it was agreed that middle managers would have to be involved as agents of change. Without them, the change just would not happen.

Lines of action

Summing up the actions taken, Sergi explained, "There are two basic lines of action: one is a new business orientation, based on a change of strategy to meet market needs; the other is a good action plan, the backbone of which is the new management system called 'management by missions.' The message from general management is that Sony España, in order to continue to exist (as a subsidiary of Sony Corporate and Sony Europe), must add value as a sales and marketing company. Economically speaking, to make a profit we have two options: to cut costs or to increase sales (or both).

Against that background, we considered what we could do qualitatively to change the situation. We decided that as far as the market was concerned we'd change our business strategy and, internally, we'd change the way we do things. So instead of using management by objectives, as we had until then, we decided to take it a step further and manage by missions. All this was accompanied by a very ambitious internal communication plan and a development plan that was absolutely crucial for changing behaviors."

	Lines of action for cultural change
Toward the market ⇒	New business strategy
Internally ⇒	New way of doing things (Management by missions)

Implementation of management by missions

Seminar at IESE

To start the project, it was decided that the company's 100 most senior managers should be involved. That amounted to practically all the people with management responsibility. This phase kicked off with a special two-day seminar on MBM, held in October 2004 at IESE.

Sergi recalled the Sony people's comments on the seminar. The reactions fell into two groups: "At last! This is what we've been waiting for" and "Here we go again! It's the usual old blather." Overall, people were skeptical. Sergi also remembered other reactions: "It's not that easy to change"; "Top management should set an example"; "I'm not going to change if my boss doesn't"; and so on. After the seminar, Juan José del Castillo thought to himself, "This was all very interesting, but what next? I mean, it's what we want to hear. It's the way things ought to be. It's what we need today."

Deploying the mission in shared missions

After the seminar, Sony España started to put MBM into practice. The first step was to create a map of shared missions. Just as the corporate mission is the reason why a company exists, the shared mission is the reason why each of the company's units, departments, and functional areas exists. In each case, the shared mission is the contribution that defines the identity of the area or department concerned.

Work began with a value chain analysis, based on Michael Porter's methods, identifying the company's primary and secondary processes. Once the company's main processes had been described, each department held working sessions, in small groups, to identify the department's value contribution to the mission. Each group organized its proposals in terms of the 3 P's of the corporate mission. In all, 22 shared missions were defined. They covered all areas of the organization and met the three basic criteria for shared missions: inclusion, complementarity, and consistency.

Together with the direct mission contribution, the working groups also identified the interdependencies among areas. In Sony, each department was asked to specify what it needed the other departments to do in order to be able to accomplish its shared mission. Then, there were discussions among the departments involved to see how things could be improved. At the end, a customer–supplier matrix was established and published, so that everybody knew the interdependencies between the different departments. Based on this matrix and through meetings among the parties, internal service commitments were established among all areas with the aim of improving cooperation in a structured, targeted way.

Sergi recalled, "At first, we had to provide the impetus. We had consultants in every day, because the first thing was to implement the overall mission, the shared missions, and the interdependencies. And all this was cascaded down through the organization to get everybody involved. We started from the corporate mission, the 3 P's; then the first level, the second level, and, in some cases, the third level. For the shared missions we stopped at the second level, always making sure the people just below the level we were working at were involved, as they were the ones who would eventually have to be motivated by that shared mission." Exhibit 10.2 shows an example of (first- and second-level) shared missions in the people dimension in one area of the company (the infrastructure department).

The MBM method slowly started to sink in at Sony España. The map of shared missions and the inter-area cooperation commitments elicited a very positive response in terms of participation and communication. They also helped people understand the ways in which the mission and the management system were consistent with one another. According to Juan José del Castillo, "Our people management department has done a very good job of explaining these concepts and each person's role. People are being made to become participants. They're being given examples, and they're being listened to in information sessions around the country. I see that the message is getting across. Basically, I don't think there's anybody in the company now who isn't

Exhibit 10.2 Example of shared missions (P for "People") on two levels

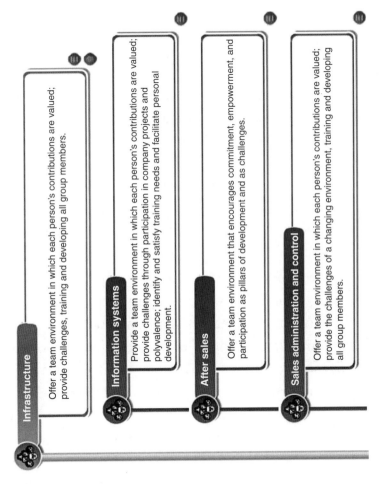

aware of this issue and who doesn't know what a shared mission is. Whether they put it into practice or not is another matter. But at least we know where we're going. And people are changing their attitudes . . . I think there are very few people who don't believe in this system. Everybody knows what the 3 P's are, and they all apply them in their decisions."

The company had made it very clear that the shared missions were not just another theoretical exercise, but would be the basic framework for employee assessment and development at Sony España. With regard to shared missions and their impact on performance assessments, Juan José del Castillo observed, "I believe much more in linking performance and development to the accomplishment of shared missions than I do in a number lifted from a budget handed down to us by European headquarters or Tokyo, or a market share target when the overall market trend may have been disastrous. It just doesn't seem fair . . . By contrast, if you make your best effort to accomplish the shared mission and you do what you know is your mission in the company, to me that seems much more satisfactory."

Once the map of shared missions and interdependencies had been finalized, implementation continued with an effort to define one or more indicators for each component of the corporate mission and shared missions. The result was the MSC (see example in Exhibit 10.3). The MSC contained indicators of

Exhibit 10.3 Mission scorecard indicators

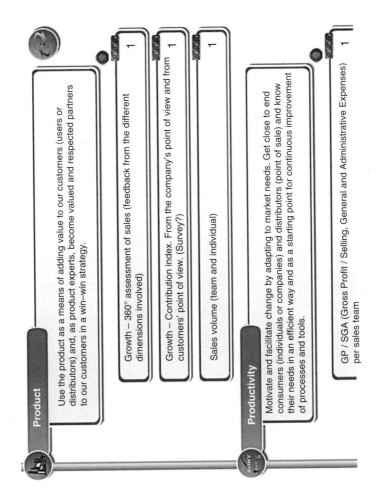

Product

Use the product as a means of adding value to our customers (users or distributors) and, as product experts, become valued and respected partners to our customers in a win–win strategy.

Growth – 360° assessment of sales (feedback from the different dimensions involved)   1

Growth – Contribution index. From the company's point of view and from customers' point of view. (Survey?)   1

Sales volume (team and individual)   1

Productivity

Motivate and facilitate change by adapting to market needs. Get close to end consumers (individuals or companies) and distributors (point of sale) and know their needs in an efficient way and as a starting point for continuous improvement of processes and tools.

GP / SGA (Gross Profit / Selling, General and Administrative Expenses) per sales team   1 different kinds, balancing financial ratios (sales, market share, productivity, profit, etc.) with nonfinancial measures (customer service, employee development, internal cooperation projects, etc.).

Wherever possible, existing indicators were used. In the people management department, for instance, various indicators were based on the regular internal customer satisfaction survey. The survey was an established management tool, but now it would have a much more specific purpose, consistent with the department's shared mission. Where there were no existing indicators, specific new ones were designed. This was done for customer satisfaction and employee development, for example.

Overall, the scorecard was built 70 percent on existing indicators and 30 percent on specific new indicators. The MSC was designed to measure, monitor, and assess progress in all aspects (financial and nonfinancial) of the corporate mission and shared missions. The fundamental point about the BSC was that, for the first time, the company had a tool derived directly from the mission to measure its overall development and progress.

Mission-linked objectives

Once the mission had been deployed to the different areas and levels of the company, Sony started to apply one of the basic principles of MBM: "a mission without objectives is a dead mission, and an objective without a mission is a blind objective." Sony redesigned its basic objectives and performance management system so as to link the existing system with the chosen missions and indicators.

Before implementing MBM, Sony had had a system of objectives in place in all areas of the company. The challenge was to build on the existing system as far as possible, while making it consistent with the mission deployment so far.

Accordingly, three types of objectives were defined: mission contribution objectives (based on the shared mission indicators); internal customer contribution objectives (based on the interdependency matrix); and development objectives (based on key mission-linked behaviors and competencies). Thus, using the existing objectives system, Sony España started to adopt the shared missions and interdependencies as the basis for annual goal setting.

Another thing that MBM contributed was the goal-setting process itself. As in the Hoshin Kanri method, each individual was responsible for setting his own objectives. His boss might have the last word, but the employee took the initiative. Whenever a Sony manager or employee set his objectives, the first question he had to ask was, "What goals must I set myself in order to make a bigger contribution to product, productivity, and people?" This meant that all objectives – whether sales department objectives or accounts department objectives – were designed to serve the company's mission.

With regard to this process, Sergi commented, "All these are tools, or means to an end, which is not so much to set good objectives (that too, of course, because if I set the right objectives, I'll improve our productivity, the way we work, and the company as a whole) as to ensure that when I set myself goals and discuss them with my boss, he has the means to coach me, and I can do the same with my own subordinates. In fact, that is the main output we're looking for here."

Combined with the goal setting process, Sony España also reoriented its performance assessment system (the counterpart of the objectives system) in the direction of integral assessment, taking into account not only "what" each person does but also "how" he does it. In a word, performance assessment came to be centered on an employee's overall contribution to the mission, which was specified along three primary axes: accomplishment of mission-aligned objectives; accomplishment of internal service improvement objectives; and development of mission-linked competencies.

Another fundamental issue with regard to the objectives system and performance assessment was how MBM related to the compensation system. Under existing company practice, some – especially turnover-related – objectives were linked to a bonus.

Other, more qualitative objectives, or those related to personal development, remained unlinked to variable pay. In Sergi's opinion, "this separation was key from the start. The objectives that are not linked to variable pay are the ones that have made it possible to promote and improve coaching and leadership in the company. These are the objectives that prevent a boss from relying entirely on the compensation system to motivate people and that force him to actively foster commitment among his team."

Mission-focused leadership

Once the mission had been deployed in shared missions and the objectives system had been redesigned, what Sony called Phase 1 of the project was complete. Phase 2, which started in parallel with Phase 1, was designed and implemented with one clear goal in mind: to develop top and middle manager leadership.

On the subject of leadership at Sony España, Sergi observed, "We had leadership problems, communication problems. To us, communication meant major announcements, emails, speeches . . . But the fact is it's day-to-day communication that really counts. And we had a lot of work to do in that area. After one year of MBM, I could see it really was a powerful tool that was going to help us achieve our final objective: to have bosses who were leaders."

"At the same time, I realized that the system was not enough on its own, that we needed something more. People needed to be trained not only in the management system, but also in this type of leadership, both things at once. Last year we focused mainly on the process, the tool: creating the map of shared missions, interdependencies, indicators, and objectives. This year (the second phase), we're learning as we go along. The most important thing is that, now, we have a coherent model, and systems and leadership both pull in the same direction. We're getting to the point where managers are starting to see this, that it's about development, about being better leaders; that it's about coaching."

Leadership training was carried out in two ways: through training and through multidisciplinary projects. A great deal of time and effort was invested in training. It wasn't done in short, intense bursts, but rather as a "steady fine rain." Right from the start, the whole workforce was involved in various training actions over the year. The ultimate goal of this training was to develop leadership. Specifically, it was centered on the three pillars of mission-focused leadership: commitment, cooperation, and change.

The second means of developing leadership consisted of multidisciplinary improvement projects. These were projects carried out by people from different departments, aimed at improving productivity, workplace climate, work-life balance, and so on. At the end of these projects, Sergi declared, "We got three outputs from these projects: the result of the project itself; breaking silos, which led to more networking; and better leadership."

Many employees even seized the opportunity to join social volunteering projects in their free time. In Francisco Juan's opinion, "In terms of our 3 P's, we were neglecting the P for people. Helping NGOs and other organizations in our spare time has made us better people. And I think there's a direct relationship between that and being better professionals. Also, these projects are very enriching, because you're working with colleagues from other divisions; and that's one of the most important things, because maybe we were too focused on commercial interests. This makes us see things in a new light, as colleagues and as a company. We see things differently. In fact, I've changed my management style. I thought it would be difficult, being older and more set in my ways. But there's one thing I'm doing a lot more, and that's listening to people. . . . Another thing I'm trying to change in my way of managing is to add a drop of humor."

At the end of Phase 2, Sergi declared, "Today I realize even more clearly just how badly we needed to get to work on this Phase 2, to develop leadership. With Phase 1 we aroused a lot of people's interest and enthusiasm, but the real change doesn't happen until people take it to heart. And that's where leadership is crucial. All the effort we've put into training is bearing fruit. We're seeing improvements in every area of the company."

Results

With respect to the current situation, Francisco Juan said, "There's a new atmosphere in the organization, we're on the right track. We're not the same people any more, either in the way we see things or in the way we behave. We've got to a position where almost the entire workforce are more interested in what other people around them are doing. Now, we all know what everybody else is doing. I even get stopped in the corridors, with people asking me, 'How are we doing, Paco? How are we doing this month? Are we on target to accomplish the mission?' "

Juanjo added, "Today, the project is gradually gaining in credibility. Right from the start there were a lot of people who believed in it. Others had their doubts, but now they're coming around. In the last six months, a lot of people who didn't believe in it have started to believe. They can see the changes. They can see that the company is listening to them." Regarding outstanding issues, he added, "We need to see a lot more things being done on a daily basis, not just in meetings or every few days, but daily and over the long term. Then we'll see it reflected in all our employees. It's not easy, but we're improving. People are making serious efforts. As soon as the top-, first-, and second-level managers all start pulling in the same direction, it'll be a sign that everybody believes in what we're doing. Because at the end of the day you always want to see if your boss is acting any differently now from the way he used to. Right now maybe 80 percent or 90 percent of the workforce agree with this way of working. That still leaves 10 percent who are, like, OK but they need to work at it five days a week, not just two or three. Consistency at all levels, that's what we need."

On a general level, Sergi noted, "As of today, the project outcome can be summed up in terms of the achievements, both in implementing the new business strategy and in establishing the new way of doing things. If we look at the mission, the results are plain to see in every area.

As regards the first of our 3 Ps, 'Add value to the Product,' the sales, profit, and market share indicators have risen steadily in recent years. At the same time, Sony España has established itself as a key player within Sony Europe. Last year, besides the President Award and the Sales Manager Award, we were the leader in Europe in the ranking of KPIs for European excellence (FuKatsu).

As regards the P for Productivity, the efficiency indicators have also improved considerably, and there's a widespread feeling in the company that permanent change is the key to continuous improvement. We're getting to a position where each person, in his job, suggests ways of doing things differently and better. One of the results has been a drop in the ratio of expenses to sales in a relatively short time, taking us to near the top of the league in Sony Europe and making us the most profitable company.

The P for People was perhaps the one that was taken least seriously until the cultural change started. The improvement since then has been spectacular. The workplace climate surveys have improved year after year, leaving us in little doubt as to whether we chose the right strategy. And there's no doubt in our minds that having all the people in this company involved has been key to getting such good results in all three P's.

Of course, we still have a long way to go. Or rather, we know we're headed in the right direction, even though we still have a long way to go. MBM offers a wide range of possibilities, and our leadership style is starting to become established. But I doubt we've done more than 40 percent of what we could do. Even so, the key ratios and survey results have shot up, so we must be doing something right. That's very encouraging and gives us strength to continue."

Afterword

There is no denying that many companies have tried to create a high-commitment culture, even allocating funds to that purpose. In most cases, however, their efforts have produced training and communication programs that are unequal to the task at hand. The root of the problem is that none of these attempts has substantially altered the management system, which continues to be strongly focused on each person's or department's economic objectives. This system has severe limitations when it comes to building shared commitment. Eventually, it leads to noncooperation, up and down the command chain and across the organization.

We have found that many companies diagnose this problem as "bad internal communication" or "lack of team work." Having worked with companies on these issues for several years, we have come to the conclusion that, although the symptoms must be addressed, the treatment will not be effective unless it goes to the root of the problem. In our opinion, effective treatment requires a far-reaching change in two fundamental respects: (1) the company's management systems; and (2) the leadership style of its executives and middle managers. The change in these two dimensions must be coordinated, based on a common project that has the necessary content, credibility, and sense of urgency.

This is the change we aim to bring about through management by missions. It is not a quick or easy solution, much less a panacea that will take effect without the need for ongoing commitment and effort by top management. Turning a deeply disaffected workforce into a cohesive and committed organization requires a revolution in every area of the company. It is a transformation that involves breaking with practices and paradigms that are deeply embedded in many companies' culture and management systems, and ingrained in their managers' style of leadership. It is unlikely to be achieved through internal communication programs, however creative.

In this book, we have merely outlined the main concepts of MBM (starting with the more theoretical premises and ending with some basic tools). In fact, we have merely skimmed the surface, as anyone who tries to put MBM into practice in their company will discover. We have written very little about how to actually implement MBM. Intentionally, we have ignored such things as change management techniques, how to design a communication plan, scheduling, process mapping and value chain analysis, leadership competency development, goal deployment, or common problem-solving tactics for implementation projects. All these aspects, though important, are beyond the scope of this book.

Moreover, there are more fundamental issues for which we still have no definitive answer. For example, what will happen when more and more companies have a mission-driven workforce? From what we have seen to date, these companies excel in areas such as customer service, recruitment, and retention of high caliber employees, and swift strategy implementation, and it becomes impossible for other companies to compete in their area or industry. Mission-driven organizations change the rules of the game in the market. However, this effect is gradual and is only just the beginning. It will probably be decades before we can judge the impact on the economy as a whole.

How a mission-driven conception of the company will affect society is another interesting question. A growth in corporate social responsibility (CSR) is one of the first results we can see today. But in a paradigm change of this kind, that may be just the tip of the iceberg. After all, CSR is largely a consequence of corporate decisions heavily influenced by considerations of image and marketing. The real change will take place when the demand for social responsibility toward stakeholders comes not only from top management but from all the employees of the company.

As we said earlier, reaching a mission-driven organization is still a major challenge for most companies. The time is ripe, and the new era of the "worker in search of meaning" – people's need to work in an enterprise that has a rich and motivating mission – favors change. True leaders are those who build organizations of people who are genuinely committed to a particular mission and certain values. To do this, they must have determination and the courage to overcome some of the paradigms embodied in management systems inherited from the past. They are the ones who will decide the rules of the game with respect to many of the most important economic and social issues of coming decades.

Notes

1   Is there a link between corporate culture and profit?

1. J. Pfeffer, *The Human Equation*. Boston, MA: Harvard Business School Press, 1998.
2. A. de Geus, "The Living company." *Harvard Business Review* (March–April 1997).
3. T. Peters and R. Waterman, *In Search of Excellence*. New York: Harper & Row, 1982.
4. R.B. Shaw, *Trust in the Balance*. San Francisco: Jossey-Bass Publishers, 1997.
5. C. Handy, "The Citizen Corporation." *Harvard Business Review* (September–October 1997).
6. S. Ghoshal and C.A. Bartlett, *The Individualized Corporation*. New York: Harper Business, 1997.
7. J. Meyer and N. Allen, *Commitment in the Workplace*. Thousand Oaks, CA: Sage, 1997.
8. R. Simons, "HP project manager." In R.B. Shaw, Ed., *Trust in the Balance*. San Francisco: Jossey-Bass Publishers, 1997, p. 4.
9. Ghoshal and Bartlett, *The Individualized Corporation*, p. 93.
10. ServiceMaster, 1995 Annual Report (Downers Grove, Illinois). Quoted in Pfeffer, op. cit., p. 298.
11. J.P. Kotter and J.L. Heskett, *Corporate Culture and Performance*. New York: The Free Press, 1992.
12. The measure of unity was constructed with the normalized average score of five statements, each scored from 1 (strongly disagree) to 7 (strongly agree):

    1. The company has a corporate purpose that employees know and are enthusiastic about.
    2. The company has important, known medium and long-term goals other than financial ones.
    3. The company's key employees have complete trust in top management.

4. There is a high degree of cooperation among all employees.

5. Employees are deeply committed to the company's mission and goals.

The measure of unity met the appropriate reliability criteria, with a Cronbach alpha of 0.84.

13. M.L. Tushman and C.A. O'Reilly III, *Winning through Innovation*. Boston, MA: Harvard Business School Press, 1997, p. 49.

2   Different ways of understanding an organization

1. F.W. Taylor, *The Principles of Scientific Management*. New York: Harper & Row, 1915.

2. H. Fayol, *General and Industrial Management*. New York: Pitman Publishing Corporation, 1949.

3. D. McGregor, *The Human Side of Enterprise*. New York: McGraw Hill, 1960.

4. J. Pfeffer, *The Human Equation*. Boston, MA: Harvard Business School Press, 1998.

5. P. Drucker, "Management by Objectives and Self-Control." *The Practice of Management*. New York: Harper & Row, 1954, Chapter 11.

6. G.S. Odiorne, *Management by Objectives*. New York: Pitman Publishing Corporation, 1965, p. 56.

7. P. Drucker, *Managing for Results*. New York: Harper & Row, 1964.

8. E. Lawler, *Rewarding Excellence*. San Francisco, CA: Jossey-Bass, 2000.

9. W. Ouchi, *Theory Z: How American Business Can Meet the Japanese Challenge*. Reading, MA: Addison-Wesley, 1981.

10. R.T. Pascale and A. Althos, *The Art of Japanese Management*. New York: Simon & Schuster, 1981.

11. T. Peters and R. Waterman, *In Search of Excellence*. New York: Harper & Row, 1982.

12. C.I. Barnard, *The Functions of the Executive*. Cambridge, MA: Harvard University Press, 1938.

13. The integral model of the organization is an adaptation of the ideas of Juan Antonio Pérez-López. See, for example,

the first chapter of J.A. Pérez-López, *Teoría de la Acción Humana en las Organizaciones* (Madrid: Ediciones Rialp, 1991). Although we have made some changes, this adaptation is intended to be faithful to Pérez López's account of the anthropological foundations of the company.

3 What are companies for?

1. In this chapter, rather than expounding a theory of corporate purpose, we aim merely to reflect on what companies are for. Further thoughts on this issue can be found in:

   - M. Friedman, *Capitalism and Freedom*. Chicago, IL: University of Chicago Press, 1962.
   - E. Freeman and D. Gilbert, *Corporate Strategy and the Search for Ethics*. Englewood Cliffs, NJ: Prentice Hall, 1988.
   - J.A. Pérez-López, *Fundamentos de la Dirección de Empresas*. Madrid: Ediciones Rialp, 1991.

2. C.I. Barnard, *The Functions of the Executive*. Cambridge, MA: Harvard University Press, 1938, p. 86.
3. D. Packard, speech given on March 8, 1960.
4. Friedman, *Capitalism and Freedom*.
5. See, for example, the editorial article in *The Economist* (January 22, 2005).
6. J.C. Collins and J.I. Porras, *Built to Last*. London: Century Business, 1996, p. 55.
7. P. Murphy, *Eighty Exemplary Ethics Statements*. Notre Dame, IN: University of Notre Dame Press, 1998.
8. P. Jones and L. Kahaner, *Say It and Live It: Fifty Corporate Mission Statements that Hit the Mark*. New York: Currency Doubleday, 1995.
9. M. Muckian and M.A. Arnold, "CEO Network '89." *Credit Union Management*, 12 (December 1989).
10. Ibid.
11. N. Chinchilla and J.A. Pérez López, Business or Enterprise? Different Approaches for the Management of People in Organizations. IESE, technical note FHN-216, 1990.
12. P.M. Senge, "The practice of innovation." *Leader to Leader* 9 (summer 1998).

4 Cultural problems today

1. T. Peters and R. Waterman, *In Search of Excellence*. New York: Harper & Row, 1982.
2. P. Drucker, *The Practice of Management*. New York: Harper & Row, 1954. p. 132.
3. C.I. Barnard, *The Functions of the Executive*. Cambridge, MA: Harvard University Press, 1938, p. 86.
4. W.E. Deming, *Out of the Crisis*. Cambridge, MA: MIT CAES, 1982, p. 102.

5 What is a company's mission?

1. P. Jones and L. Kahaner, *Say It and Live It: 50 Corporate Mission Statements that Hit the Mark*. New York: Currency Doubleday, 1995.
2. A. Campbell and L. Nash, *A Sense of Mission: Defining Direction for the Large Corporation*. New York: Addison-Wesley, 1992.
3. P. Drucker, *The Practice of Management*. New York: Harper & Row, 1954.
4. J.A. Pérez López, *Fundamentos de la Dirección de Empresas*. Madrid: Ediciones Rialp, 1991.
5. R. Simons, "Control in the Age of Empowerment." *Harvard Business Review* (March–April 1995).
6. P. Drucker, *Management: Tasks, Responsibilities, Practices*. New York: Harper & Row, 1974.
7. R. Clark, "Making the Corporate Mission Possible." *CA Magazine* 119 (June 1986).
8. M. Muckian and M.A. Arnold, "CEO Network '89." *Credit Union Management* 12 (December 1989).
9. Campbell and Nash, *A Sense of Mission*. New York: Addison-Wesley, 1992.
10. P. Senge, "The Practice of Innovation." *Leader to Leader* 9 (summer 1998).
11. P. Cardona and C. Rey, "Management by missions: how to make the mission a part of management." IESE occasional paper no. 03/11 (March 2003).
12. In many cases, these incomplete definitions are due to confusion between "mission" and "vision."

13. E. Freeman and D. Reed, "Stockholders and Stakeholders: A New Perspective on Corporate Governance." *California Management Review* 15(3) (spring 1983).
14. J. Pfeffer, *The Human Equation*. Boston, MA: Harvard Business School Press, 1998.
15. Ibid.
16. J.P. Kotter and J.L. Heskett, *Corporate Culture and Performance*. New York: The Free Press, 1992.
17. Having warned of the dangers of "How to write a mission statement" manuals, any reader who would like to explore the subject further might be interested in the following titles:

    – Six Rules for Writing and Implementing Your Own Mission Statement. Jones and Kahaner, *Say It and Live It*.
    – How to write a mission statement. J. Abrahams, *The Mission Statement Book: 301 Mission Statements from America's Top Companies*. Berkeley, CA: Ten Speed Press, 1999.
    – Do You Have a Good Mission Statement? Campbell and Nash, *A Sense of Mission*.

6 The values of a balanced culture

1. S. García and S. Dolan, *Dirección por valores*. Madrid: McGraw-Hill, 1997.
2. P. Murphy, *Eighty Exemplary Ethics Statements*. Notre Dame, IN: University of Notre Dame Press, 1998.
3. J.C. Collins and J.I. Porras, *Built to Last: Successful Habits of Visionary Companies*. London: Century Business, 1996.
4. Fifty-four values (8% of the sample) that could not be classified into any of the four categories or that could belong to more than one category were discarded.
5. T.E. Deal and A.A. Kennedy, *Corporate Cultures*. Addison-Wesley, 1982.

7 The mission chart

1. For a more detailed discussion of the managerial mission, see J.A. Pérez-López. *Liderazgo y ética en la dirección de empresas*. Bilbao: Deusto 1998, Chapter 3.

2. W. Edwards Deming, *The New Economics*. MIT, 1994. Another detailed account of interdependency relationships is to be found in R.T. Pascale, *The Art of Japanese Management*. New York: Simon & Schuster, 1981, Chapter 5.

3. M. Hammer and J. Champy, *Reengineering the Corporation: A Manifesto for Business Revolution*. New York: Harper Business, 1993.

4. R. Kaplan and D. Norton, *The Balanced Scorecard*. Boston, MA: Harvard Business School Press, 1996, p. 33.

5. S. Covey, *The 7 Habits of Highly Effective People*. New York: Simon & Shuster, 1990.

6. For a fuller discussion of the personal mission and its relevance to the field of competencies, see P. Cardona and P. García-Lombardía, *Cómo Desarrollar las Competencias de Liderazgo*. Pamplona: EUNSA, 2005.

7. S. Covey, *First Things First*. New York: Simon & Shuster, 1992.

8 Mission management tools

1. W.E. Deming, *The New Economics for Industry, Government, Education*. Cambridge, MA: MIT, 1994.

2. G.W. George, "Academy Address." *Academy of Management Executive* 15(4) (2001).

3. J.G. Johnson and K. Scholes, *Exploring Corporate Strategy*. Englewood Cliffs, NJ: Prentice Hall, 2001.

4. C.P. Cardona and P. García-Lombardía, *How to develop leadership competencies*. Pamplona: EUNSA, 2005.

5. C. Woodrufe, *Assessment Centers: Identifying and Developing Competences*. London: Institute of Personnel Management, 1993.

6. M. Vilallonga (ed.), *Coaching Directivo: Desarrollando el Liderazgo*. Barcelona: Ariel, 2003.

9 Mission-driven leadership

1. J.C. Rost, *Leadership for the Twenty-First Century*. New York: Praeger, 1991.

2. P. Cardona, "Transcendental leadership." *The Leadership & Organization Development Journal* 21(4) (2000): 201–206.

3. B.M. Bass and B.J. Avolio, *Improving Organizational Effect-iveness through Transformational Leadership.* Thousand Oaks, CA: Sage, 1994, p. 3.

4. W.G. Bennis, *On Becoming a Leader.* Reading, MA: Addison-Wesley, 1989.

5. M. Maccoby, "Narcissistic Leaders: The Incredible Pros, the Inevitable Cons." *Harvard Business Review* (January 2000).

6. B.M. Bass and P. Steidlmeier, "Ethics, Character, and Auth-entic Transformational Leadership Behavior." *Leadership Quarterly* 10(2) (1999): 181–217.

7. J. Collins comes to the same conclusions in Level 5 Leader-ship: The Triumph of Humility and Fierce Resolve, *Harvard Business Review* (January 2001).

8. C.I. Barnard, *The Functions of the Executive.* Cambridge, MA: Harvard University Press, 1938.

9. Although in practice it is possible to cooperate for other motives, such as money (extrinsic motives), such motivation is not sufficient to ensure sustainable cooperation.

10. The issue of internal customer–supplier relationships has been studied and discussed in various publications since the 1980s. To know more about the systems and tools that can facilitate this process, we recommend reading a good TQM manual.

11. Also known as Service Level Agreements (SLAs).

12. J.G. March, Exploration and Exploitation in Organizational Learning, *Organization Science* 2(1) (1991): 71–87.

Bibliography

Abrahams, J. *The Mission Statement Book: 301 Mission Statements from America's Top Companies*. Berkeley, CA: Ten Speed Press, 1999.

Barnard, C.I. *The Functions of the Executive*. Cambridge, MA: Harvard University Press, 1938.

Bass, B.M. and B.J. Avolio. *Improving Organizational Effectiveness Through Transformational Leadership*. Thousand Oaks, CA: Sage, 1994.

Bass, B.M. and P. Steidlmeier. "Ethics, Character, and Authentic Transformational Leadership Behavior." *Leadership Quarterly* 10(2) (1999): 181–217.

Batson, C.D. *The Altruism Question*. Hillsdale, NJ: Lawrence Erlbaum Associates, 1991.

Bennis, W.G. *On Becoming a Leader*. Reading, MA: Addison-Wesley, 1989.

Block, P. *Stewardship: Choosing Service over Self-interest*. San Francisco, CA: Berrett-Koehler Publishers, 1993.

Campbell, A. and L. Nash. *A Sense of Mission: Defining Direction for the Large Corporation*. New York: Addison-Wesley, 1992.

Cardona, P. "Transcendental Leadership." *The Leadership & Organization Development Journal* 21(4) (2000): 201–206.

Cardona, P. and P. Garcia-Lombardía. *Cómo Desarrollar las Competencias de Liderazgo*. Pamplona: EUNSA, 2005.

Cardona, P. and C. Rey. Dirección por Misiones: Cómo Introducir la Misión en la Gestión. IESE occasional paper no. 03/11, March 2003.

Cardona, P., B. Lawrence, and P.M. Bentler. "The Influence of Social and Work Exchange Relationships on Organizational Citizenship Behavior." *Group and Organization Management* 29(2) (2004): 219–247.

Chinchilla N. and J.A. Pérez López. Empresa o Negocio? Distintos Enfoques para la Dirección de Personas. IESE, technical note FHN-216, 1990.

Clark, R. "Making the Corporate Mission Possible." *CA Magazine* 119 (June 1986).

Collins, J.C. and J.I. Porras. *Built to Last: Successful Habits of Visionary Companies*. London: Century Business, 1996.

Covey, S. *The 7 Habits of Highly Effective People*. New York: Simon & Shuster, 1990.

Covey, S. *First Things First*. New York: Simon & Shuster, 1992.

Deal, T. and A. Kennedy. *Corporate Cultures: The Rites and Rituals of Corporate Life*. Reading, MA: Addison-Wesley, 1982.

De Geus, A. "The Living Company." *Harvard Business Review* (March–April 1997).

Deming, W.E. *Out of the Crisis*. Cambridge, MA: MIT CAES, 1982.

Deming, W.E. *The New Economics for Industry, Government, Education*. Cambridge, MA: MIT, 1994.

Drucker, P. *The Practice of Management*. New York: Harper & Row, 1954.

Drucker, P. *Managing for Results*. New York: Harper & Row, 1964.

Drucker, P. *Management: Tasks, Responsibilities, Practices*. New York: Harper & Row, 1974.

Fayol, H. *General and Industrial Management*. New York: Pitman Publishing Corporation, 1949.

Freeman, E. and D. Gilbert. *Corporate Strategy and the Search for Ethics*. Englewood Cliffs, NJ: Prentice Hall, 1988.

Freeman, E. and D. Reed. "Stockholders and Stakeholders: A New Perspective on Corporate Governance." *California Management Review* 25(3) (Spring 1983).

Friedman, M. *Capitalism and Freedom*. Chicago, IL: University of Chicago Press, 1962.

García S. and S. Dolan. *Dirección por Valores. El Cambio Más Allá de la DPO*. Madrid: McGraw-Hill, 1997.

George, W. "Academy Address." *Academy of Management Executive* 15(4) (2001).

Ghoshal, S. and C.A. Bartlett. *The Individualized Corporation*. New York: Harper Business, 1997.

Gini, A. "Too Much to Say about Something." *Business Ethics Quarterly* 5(1) (1995): 143–155.

Gouldner, A.W. "The Norm of Reciprocity." *American Sociological Review* 25 (1960): 161–178.

Greenleaf, R.K. *The Servant as a Leader*. Indianapolis, IN: The Greenleaf Center, 1970.

Hammer, M. and J. Champy. *Reengineering the Corporation: A Manifesto for Business Revolution.* New York: Harper Business, 1993.

Handy, C. "The Citizen Corporation." *Harvard Business Review* (September–October 1997).

Johnson G. and K. Scholes. *Exploring Corporate Strategy.* 7th edition. Englewood Cliffs, NJ: Prentice Hall, 2001.

Jones, P. and L. Kahaner. *Say It and Live It: 50 Corporate Mission Statements that Hit the Mark.* New York: Currency Doubleday, 1995.

Kaplan, R. and D. Norton. *The Balanced Scorecard.* Boston, MA: Harvard Business School Press, 1996.

Kotter, J.P. and J.L. Heskett. *Corporate Culture and Performance.* New York: The Free Press, 1992.

Lawler, E. *Rewarding Excellence.* San Francisco, CA: Jossey-Bass, 2000.

Maccoby, M. "Narcissistic Leaders: The Incredible Pros, the Inevitable Cons." *Harvard Business Review* (January–February 2000).

McGregor, D. *The Human Side of Enterprise.* New York: McGraw Hill, 1960.

Meyer, J. and N. Allen. *Commitment in the Workplace.* Thousand Oaks, CA: Sage, 1997.

Muckian, M. and M.A. Arnold. "CEO Network '89." *Credit Union Management* (12 December 1989).

Murphy, P. *Eighty Exemplary Ethics Statements.* Notre Dame, IN: University of Notre Dame Press, 1998.

Odiorne, G. *Management by Objectives.* New York: Pitman Publishing Corporation, 1965.

Ouchi, W. *Theory Z: How American Business can Meet the Japanese Challenge.* Reading, MA: Addison-Wesley, 1981.

Pascale, R.T. *The Art of Japanese Management.* New York: Simon & Schuster, 1981.

Pérez López, J.A. *Fundamentos de la Dirección de Empresas.* Madrid: Ediciones Rialp, 1991.

Pérez López, J.A. *Paradigmas del Liderazgo.* Madrid: Ediciones Rialp, 1991.

Pérez-López, J.A. *Teoría de la Acción Humana en las Organizaciones.* Madrid: Ediciones Rialp, 1991.

Pérez López, J.A. *Liderazgo y Ética en la Dirección de Empresas.* Bilbao: Deusto, 1998.

Peters, T. and R. Waterman. *In Search of Excellence*. New York: Harper & Row, 1982.

Pfeffer, J. *The Human Equation*. Boston, MA: Harvard Business School Press, 1998.

Rost, J.C. *Leadership for the Twenty-First Century*. New York: Praeger, 1991.

Senge, P. "The Practice of Innovation." *Leader to Leader* 9 (Summer 1998).

Shaw, R.B. *Trust in the Balance*. San Francisco, CA: Jossey-Bass Publishers, 1997.

Simons, R. "Control in the Age of Empowerment." *Harvard Business Review* (March–April 1995).

Staw, B. and L.L. Cummings (eds). *Research in Organizational Behavior*. Greenwich, CT: JAI Press, 1993.

Taylor, F.W. *The Principles of Scientific Management*. New York: Harper & Row, 1915.

Tushman, M.L. and C.A. O'Reilly III. *Winning through Innovation*. Boston, MA: Harvard Business School Press, 1997.

Vilallonga, M. (ed.). *Coaching Directivo: Desarrollando el Liderazgo*. Barcelona: Ariel, 2003.

Vroom, V.H. *Work and Motivation*. New York: John Wiley & Sons, Inc., 1964.

Woodrufe, C. *Assessment Centers: Identifying and Developing Competences*. London: Institute of Personnel Management, 1993.

Index

In this index tables, figures, exhibits and notes are indicated in italics, enclosed in parenthesis, following the page number. E.g. aggregated, 57(*fig.4.2*). Notes are indicated by *n*. Tables by tab. Figures by fig. Works are entered in italics.